eat vegan on $4 a day

A GAME PLAN FOR THE BUDGET-CONSCIOUS COOK

Ellen Jaffe Jones

BOOK PUBLISHING COMPANY
Summertown Tennessee

Library of Congress Cataloging-in-Publication Data

Jones, Ellen Jaffe.
    Eat vegan on $4 a day : a game plan for the budget-conscious cook /
Ellen Jaffe Jones.
        p. cm.
    Includes index.
    ISBN 978-1-57067-257-6 (pbk.) -- ISBN 978-1-57067-980-3 (e-book)
 1. Vegan cooking. 2. Low budget cooking. 3. Cookbooks. I. Title.
 II. Title: Eat vegan on four dollars a day.
    TX837.J5428 2011
    641.5'52—dc23

                                                    2011011974

Cover and interior design: John Wincek

Book Publishing Company
P.O. Box 99
Summertown, TN 38483
888-260-8458
www.bookpubco.com

ISBN: 978-1-57067-257-6

Printed in The United States of America

17 16 15 14 13 12 11   9 8 7 6 5 4 3 2

Book Publishing Company is a member of Green Press Initiative. We chose to print this title on paper with 100% post consumer recycled content, processed without chlorine, which saves the following natural resources:

    49 trees
    1,421 pounds of solid waste
    22,415 gallons of water
    4,971 pounds of greenhouse gases
    20 million BTU of energy

For more information on Green Press Initiative, visit www.greenpressinitiative.org.

Environmental impact estimates were made using the Environmental Defense Fund Paper Calculator. For more information visit www.papercalculator.org.

Printed on recycled paper

contents

acknowledgments

To John McDougall, MD, for his tireless passion over the years to keep singing the same song. I have read all his books, but it was a simple sentence he wrote in an old newsletter filled with recipes that spoke to me. He said all of the recipes could be made for $3 a day. Wow! Really? And so began my journey to prove him right.

To Neal Barnard, MD, and all the doctors and registered dietitians at The Cancer Project and Physicians Committee for Responsible Medicine (PCRM). They are my heroes for standing up to big money and politics in the best interest of our health and our children. Some of my recipes have been adapted from The Cancer Project to show that you don't have to spend a bundle to eat well.

To the folks at Vitamix, who, by inventing a great blender decades ago, made healthful eating for me as a single, working mom so much easier.

To Patti Breitman, who wanted this book to be published with a passion equal to mine. Her guidance and knowledge were gifts from heaven. Her belief in my thoughts and words kept me on track.

To my editor, Caroline Pincus, who is as swift and on target as the best surgeon.

To Jo Stepaniak, whose books have inspired me over many years. I feel deeply honored to have had her as my editor at Book Publishing Company. Beth Geisler was also a gift. Bountiful gratitude goes to Cynthia Holzapfel at Book Publishing Company for believing in my vision that if you show people how easy it is to save money by eating healthfully, they will flock to the table.

To the many websites that educate about environmental issues and plant-based eating. Our future may depend on our ability to connect the dots between what is good for our bodies and what is good for our planet's survival.

To the community leaders in Bradenton, Florida, and everywhere else, who have the courage and dedication to run community supported farms.

To the students who have attended my cooking classes and the children I have had the honor of coaching, especially the Manatec County, Florida, high school girls track and cross-country teams. I received way more information, inspiration, and ideas from you than you'll ever know.

To my friends in running clubs everywhere. Your secrets are safe with me. I hope mine are safe with you too.

To so many friends and relatives who didn't live to see this day. Memories of you still live on and ignite inspiration.

To my mom, who was always there to listen and loved when I picked dandelions for her. She would chuckle to know that I eat them now. And my dad, who marveled at nature daily, had beautiful backyard gardens, and made me pull weeds instead of spraying them. I've tried to honor one of his many quotable quotes: "I calls 'em as I sees 'em."

To my three daughters, who endured great challenges, including nontraditional birthday cakes. Their fearlessness beyond their years was the spark that seriously ignited this book. I fervently hope that I'll be there for them if and when they have children, and that their children won't be swimming upstream to beat the odds of a bad family health history or a world plagued with preventable diseases.

To my dear husband and the love of my life, Clarence, who read the Serenity Prayer to me so many times during a family crisis that he finally plastered it on several walls. His calmness, peacefulness, and personal serenity give hope to those who think that smart and kind don't coexist in soul mates.

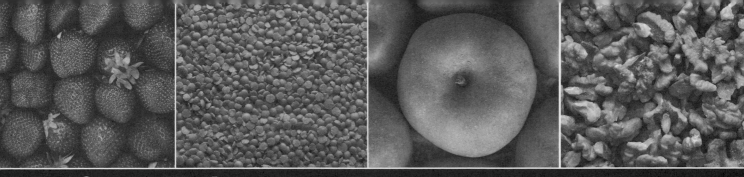

foreword

In the past few years, we have seen a decline in our economy and standard of living that many say is the worst since the stock market crash of 1929 and the following Great Depression. There may be no food lines or formal rationing like there was way back then, but good-quality health care is still informally rationed to the wealthy or fortunate who can afford or find it. Good-quality, health-promoting food has been thought to be available only at higher-priced health food stores. As belt-tightening becomes a way of life, the mad dash is on to find ways to eat well without breaking the bank.

Fortunately, even with grocery prices inching upward, for less than the amount of daily food stamp rationings, you can easily make serious dents in your food budget and improve your health dramatically. I have been researching and advocating a plant-based diet for twenty-five years, and I know it can be done. You don't have to make sudden, sweeping changes to how you eat. Even incorporating a few plant-based meals into your week will go a long way toward improving your health and your family's bottom line.

I first met Ellen Jaffe Jones years ago when she transitioned from successful consecutive careers as an Emmy Award–winning TV consumer and investigative reporter and a financial consultant at a major Wall Street firm. She had decided to join her husband in his media-consulting business, and I found their knowledge of how to deal with the media invaluable. The two of them have won the highest awards in broadcast news.

Over the years, Ellen's passion for improving health blossomed as she became a trained cooking instructor for The Cancer Project and a trained, certified coach for the Road Runners Club of America. She can run an eight-minute mile or a marathon and hold a plank position for six minutes. She also helps to coach a high school track and cross-country team and is a nationally certified personal trainer. All plant-powered. She has taken on the task of teaching people of all ages how to eat for optimum health. Defining what a healthful lifestyle would be to avoid a huge family history of disease was and continues to be her personal and professional lifelong mission. After losing her parents and several other family members to cancer, heart disease, and diabetes, figuring out how to avoid the same family fate became the investigative reporting job of her life.

Ellen's knowledge of nutrition is deep. While no formal degrees ring after her name, her cooking class evaluations and people who have heard her lectures often state, "It would take me a lifetime to know and understand what she knows." The lives and deaths of many friends and relatives have taught her well. Once, at the PCRM headquarters in Washington, DC, Ellen walked through our library of nutrition books, laughing and saying, "I believe I have all of these at home." The woman has an encyclopedic knowledge of food and food pricing.

One of the things I admire so much about Ellen is that, unlike so many people today, she is not trying to sell any product, device, or gimmick. Her goal is not to make money but to reveal the truth. When she came to me with the idea of a recipe book that would show just how easy and inexpensive it is to eat healthfully and well, I was amazed. To my knowledge, no one else has done this. No one else has written a broad-spectrum recipe book that takes into account the cost by ingredient and cost per serving. And certainly there is no one better qualified to write this book than Ellen Jaffe Jones.

What you find within these pages may surprise you, as you discover that you really can eat well—and keep yourself healthy—on just $4 a day.

NEAL D. BARNARD, MD

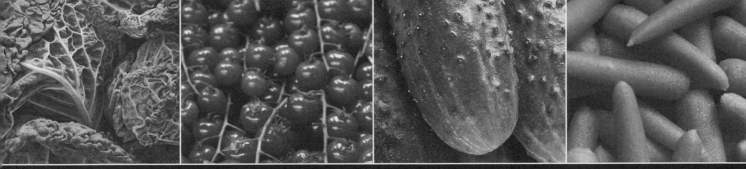

introduction

YOU *CAN* MAKE ENDS MEET

If those daily stories on the Internet or in your favorite magazines are to be believed, you can't eat healthfully *and* inexpensively. The media tell us that eating a nutritious diet costs big bucks. Fortunately, these doomsayers are wrong. This book will show you how you can eat well—really well—for a lot less than you think.

Before becoming a cooking teacher and chef, I spent eighteen years doing investigative reporting on television. Then I became a financial consultant at one of Wall Street's largest companies. I left Wall Street in 2003 to join my husband in his successful media-consulting business and began teaching cooking classes. What started out as a little passion of mine—teaching people how easy it is to prepare delicious, healthful, inexpensive meals at home—became a full-fledged, concurrent second career.

A lot of what I learned as a reporter and financial consultant has made its way into this book. For example, most people think that buying fast food is the least-expensive way to eat, but a simple investigation of the facts reveals just how wrong that is.

At today's prices, your average fast food meal would cost, say, $5. That might even be conservative, but humor me. Let's figure $2 for a large box of fries and $3 for a whopping big burger with cheese. If you want a drink, you may need to hold the cheese. Okay, breakfast may cost less, dinner may cost more. Still, in all, over the course of a year, a regimen of fast food would break down as follows:

- $5 per meal × 3 meals per day = $15 per day
- $15 per day × 365 days = $5,475 per year

So, you get the picture. The calculations above show that in just one year, one person would pay $5,475 (that's more than $450 each month) for so-called "cheap" food. On my plan you can eat *three* great-tasting, nutritious meals for less than the cost of just one of these fast food meals. And you'll be trimmer and healthier for it.

YOUR BEST BET FOR BEATING THE ODDS

These days I eat a naturally lean, whole-grain, plant-based diet. No dairy, no eggs, no meats for this girl. And I've never felt or looked better—or saved more money at the grocery store. If you're wondering why I started eating a vegan whole-foods diet, it's simple: I wanted to cheat death.

Doctors had long told me the handwriting was on the wall. My aunt died of breast cancer in our home when I was five. I almost died of a colon blockage the year my sister was diagnosed with breast cancer for the second time. When my mom and second sister got breast cancer—and I started facing the fact that every member of my family faced something life threatening, mostly heart disease and diabetes—I began reading as if my life depended on it. Many doctors told me I had to do things drastically differently than my family members. So I did. As the youngest child, I learned very well by observation what *not* to do. And I started changing my diet. Today, as the mother of three girls, I still worry about our genetic odds. But even genetic illness requires a trigger, and genetics do not dictate our destinies. There is much we can do to beat the odds.

WHAT YOU'LL FIND IN THIS BOOK

In this book I will teach you pretty much everything you need to know to eat a healthful diet for next to nothing. You'll also learn that switching to a plant-based diet isn't just about the money you will save in food costs. It's also about the long-term savings you'll realize by reducing the number of doctor visits and avoiding the costly chronic diseases that send you there in the first place. Be aware that surgeries, medical devices, and drugs may not successfully solve chronic medical problems. A healthful diet is essential to preventing and even reversing these ailments. It's up to you to take charge of your health to limit your own medical expenses and our society's soaring healthcare costs overall.

Now that food prices, along with the prices of many other consumer goods, are reaching record highs, it is time to consider financial planning for food buying as much a priority as saving for retirement. This book will give you the tools you need for planning healthful and inexpensive daily and weekly menus. You'll be able to look at one recipe, or several recipes, and easily calculate how much it will cost for one serving or multiple servings.

With each recipe, I provide the cost for one serving—as accurately as I can estimate at this moment in time.

The daily menu plans show that you really can eat nutritiously for under $4 a day—and sometimes for even less, depending on your cooking methods and ingredients. In addition to providing some serious cost savings, you'll find that my recipes taste very good. In fact, the flavor is just as impressive as the savings.

THE TWINKIES MADE ME DO IT

I had to write this book. Yes, *had to*. Here's what put me over the edge: Twinkies. I saw one too many news stories in which supermarket shoppers were asked how far a daily food-stamp allotment of $6 would get them, and they replied that they would only be able to afford foods like Twinkies and boxed macaroni and cheese. Not true! For the cost of one Twinkie, I can show you how to make six servings of delicious, high-quality, plant-based protein.

It's time for an extreme makeover of the American shopping cart. Once and for all, I'd like to dispel the myth that healthful eating is expensive or only for the elite. Every ingredient listed in this book should be available at your neighborhood grocery store—no fancy-schmancy stores required. The recipes will specify whether you should use canned, dried, fresh, or frozen ingredients. But if you don't have a choice, use whatever is available. Eat the foods and recipes recommended in this book, and you'll radiate good health—for just pennies per meal.

where are the broccoli ads?

Before I show you how to eat delicious, healthful food for only a few dollars a day, I'd like to explore how our consumer culture leads so many people to believe that junk food and convenience foods (like those Twinkies) are the most economical food choices. On a rare visit to a doctor's office recently (to check my orthotics to make sure I can keep running until I'm one hundred), I found myself thumbing through *Arthritis Today*. After spotting thirty-six ads for pharmaceuticals or medical products and services in just one edition, I stopped counting. But my curiosity was piqued, and I couldn't resist checking another edition. I flagged every page that contained a pharmaceutical-related ad.

By the time I was done, I had flagged fifty pages out of ninety. That's fifty pages of advertisements for drugs or other treatments for largely preventable diseases in just one magazine. In the small print on the third-to-last page, the magazine's publisher, the Arthritis Foundation, printed a thank-you to twenty national sponsors who "contributed $100,000 or more to support our mission." Every "sponsor" except one was a health-care provider, pharmaceutical company, or manufacturer of medical devices or arthritis supplements.

As much as I was appalled by what was in these magazines, I was struck by what was missing. Where were the recipes for whole grains and greens, which do not aggravate the body's inflammatory response and related diseases such as arthritis? Where were the recommendations for the books that patients ought to read to save themselves from frequent doctor visits? Where were the broccoli ads? Not there, of course. Why? Because there's not much money to be made from broccoli. There is no National Broccoli Association, no Broccoli Board, and no broccoli lobbyists. It's all part of a pattern that has been bringing this country down: "Success" is not about serving the greater good. Rather, it's all about the bottom line. It's all about the money, isn't it?

WHERE IS THE TRUTH?

Today the lines between advertisements and news are so blurred, even an educated consumer can find it difficult to recognize a legitimate source and message. To protect ourselves from the lies we're being told about what's best for our health, we need to ask thoughtful questions. When we see ads, we need to ask, Who paid for this? What are they *really* trying to sell me? When we see reports of scientific studies, we need to ask, Who did the scientific research? Was it unbiased research or was it junk science paid for by companies with a vested interest in the "right" outcome? Who gains from these findings? As you begin to understand who paid for the ads or the latest research that is making headlines, you will be motivated to search for untainted sources of information throughout your lifetime. As you seek answers, you will find what rings true for you and what works best for your body and wallet.

The problem is that our health-care system has conditioned us to look for a magic bullet in the form of a drug, supplement, device, or procedure to solve our medical problems. The fact is that we only need to adjust our diets and lifestyles to make our maladies fade away. If reporters were after this simple truth, every magazine, newspaper, and television news program would overflow with stories about the truly amazing benefits of eating plant-based foods. However, no person or corporation "makes" broccoli or the many health-promoting foods I'll recommend in this book, and no one stands to make a huge profit from broccoli sales. The only one who profits from vegetable sales, besides the grower, is you, the consumer, who can avoid a lifetime of medical bills and potential bankruptcy from illnesses caused by not consuming nutritious food. These are the real costs of not eating well.

Paying for illness is expensive, whether the money comes out of your pocket or the government's. The latest statistics from the American Heart Association show that more than 81 million people in the United States have one or more forms of heart disease. Every year, well over one million Americans have a new or recurring heart attack. The average total health-care cost for heart bypass surgery, per person, after five years of treatment (including the initial surgery and typical follow-up care) ranges from $100,000 to $200,000.

The reassuring news is that there is a much better bargain at the grocery store. A healthful diet can prevent and reverse not only heart disease but diabetes and cancer too. If you can avoid getting these diseases in the first place, you can really save yourself a bundle over a lifetime.

WHERE DO FOOD MARKETING DOLLARS GO?

If plant-based foods are so darned good for us, you might ask why we don't hear more about them from the government. The answer is that a great number of government policies favor the promotion of animal-based foods, such as meat and dairy, over vegan foods, such as beans, fruits, vegetables, and whole grains. Government subsidies can make some foods, such as cheeseburgers, more affordable than salads. No wonder people who have limited food budgets view the most nutritious foods as being out of reach.

The United States Department of Agriculture (USDA) plays a considerable role in how agricultural products are promoted. Although many consumers might think that this government agency exists primarily to oversee food safety and quality, the USDA must also meet the needs of food producers and market agribusiness products. Through the Checkoff Program, the USDA partners with commercial interests—such as the producers, handlers, and importers of meat, dairy products, fruits, and vegetables—to allot marketing funds for these products. For example, the Cattlemen's Beef Board and the USDA oversee the collection and spending of beef checkoff funds.

The USDA sets advertising budgets for agricultural products based on how much money is collected for them, and by far the greatest funding goes to marketing animal-based foods. Table 1 (page 4) provides a sampling of how the USDA allocates its advertising money.

As you can see from table 1, blueberries and watermelons, which are abundant in disease-fighting antioxidants and arguably two of the most nutritious commodities, are at the bottom of the list for checkoff money. Commodities such as dairy and meat, which are indisputably linked with heart disease, obesity, and the other diseases of affluence, are at the top of the food chain of promotion dollars.

TABLE 1	Advertising dollars allocated by the USDA in 2008
FOOD	**DOLLARS ALLOCATED FOR ADVERTISING**
Dairy products	$281.2 million
Fluid milk	$107.8 million
Beef	$79.8 million
Pork	$65.4 million
Hass avocados	$24.2 million
Eggs	$21 million
Potatoes	$10.7 million
Mangoes	$3.9 million
Mushrooms	$2.6 million
Lamb	$2.3 million
Blueberries	$1.9 million
Watermelons	$1.6 million

You may be surprised to know that the figures shown in table 1 don't reflect marketing efforts made by the industries themselves. We've all heard the mantra of the Cattlemen's Beef Board and National Cattlemen's Beef Association, "Beef: It's What's for Dinner," or the catchphrase promoted by the National Pork Board, "Pork: The Other White Meat." Where are the "Broccoli: It's the Cancer Killer" or "Beans: Good for Hearts and Other Parts" campaigns? These slogans never make it onto the government-produced posters that hang on the walls of our children's school cafeterias.

Okay, I think I've made my point. We're up against a lot of misinformation and disinformation, folks, and that's one of the prime reasons I wrote this book. I want to wipe away the hype. I want you to see beyond the slick advertising and deception. There's a world of fresh, wholesome, health-producing, and illness-defying foods out there that can be yours for just a few dollars a day. I can practically guarantee that the foods I recommend will cost you no more than what you are spending right now on groceries—and probably a whole lot less.

SAVING YOUR MONEY *AND* YOUR LIFE

There's also another way that following my recipes will save you money: A healthful diet based on unprocessed plant-based foods can protect you against disease and help you avoid health-care costs. If you have children, serving them a nutritious, plant-based diet is an investment in their future, setting them up for a lifetime of health-promoting habits that will help them—and their children—avoid costly trips to the doctor.

While the standard American diet, with its reliance on fast food, processed food, sugar, and especially fatty meats may seem inexpensive on the surface, it is actually quite costly. Here's why: Animal-based foods have been linked to cancer. Food animals are given foods they wouldn't normally eat and hormones they don't normally produce to make them larger and more profitable for their owners. Dairy cattle are given hormones to make them produce more milk. In addition, food animals are given feed laced with herbicides, pesticides, and other toxic chemicals that find their way into the animals' fat and muscles and ultimately into the meat, milk, and eggs people eat.

Fish and shellfish also can contain traces of dangerous substances, such as polychlorinated biphenyls (PCBs), mercury, and dichlorodiphenyltrichloroethane (DDT). PCBs, a class of industrial chemicals that were once used as coolants, electrical insulators, and lubricants, were banned in the United States in 1978. PCBs do not break down easily in the environment, however, and they can still be detected in fish that swim in polluted waters. In large amounts, PCBs can negatively affect nerve development and reproductive and hormone functions, and may cause cancer.

Mercury is a toxic metal that is naturally present in the environment. It also occurs as a result of burning coal and trash. It's found in fish in the form of methylmercury. Some fish contain more methylmercury than others; generally larger fish and those higher up in the food chain harbor greater amounts. When we eat fish, we ingest this toxin. Methylmercury can build up in our tissues, just as it does in fish, and can damage the brain, cardiovascular system, kidneys, and nerves. Fetuses, babies, and young children are most at risk because their brains develop so rapidly. All prenatal effects of exposure to mercury have been found to be permanent.

Although the pesticide DDT was banned in 1972, small amounts persist in the environment. Because DDT and its breakdown products can mimic the action of natural hormones, they may increase the chance of premature birth and reduce a mother's ability to produce milk. DDT can damage the immune system and nervous system. It is known to cause cancer in laboratory animals and may cause cancer, primarily liver and breast cancer, in humans.

So, have you lost your appetite for eggs, dairy products, and meat yet? Are you wondering if there is any way to avoid the devastating toxins in our food supply? The good news is that plant-based foods, being lower on the food chain, don't contain nearly the concentrated chemicals, contaminants, and pesticides that animal-based foods and their byproducts do.

I don't recommend a plant-based diet simply because of what plants *don't* contain, though. I recommend it because of the extras, such as fiber, that plant-based foods give us. Meat and other animal-based foods have no fiber. If you simply substitute beans for meat, you can easily increase your daily fiber consumption by twenty grams. As long as you are getting enough fiber and fluids, either from drinking water or eating water-rich fruits and vegetables, you will have a healthy colon that should never need Metamucil or any of the other of expensive fiber products that fill store shelves. You should never need the services of a colon cancer specialist.

A BRIEF NOTE ABOUT ORGANICS

The recommendation to buy organic fruits and vegetables is a good one, but it can be challenging to follow this advice if you must limit expenses. Organic produce will almost always cost more than the same foods grown conventionally. It is understandable that in a poor economy, organic food may not be on your radar, but keep the big picture in mind. If you can eat fewer foods that have pesticides on them, you may be saving money in the long run by avoiding the health problems they can cause.

If you worry about pesticides, you might wonder whether it's safer to avoid conventionally grown produce and eat meat instead. The answer is a resounding no. Animals that are raised for human consumption are given feed that is treated with chemicals and pesticides, and these become concentrated in the animals' fatty tissues. As a result, far greater amounts of these toxins are found in meat than in plants. Alarming levels of toxins are also found in fish. For example, the contamination of oysters, salmon, and other fish in Puget Sound and Chesapeake Bay by PCBs and pesticide runoff has been well documented.

The best approach is to reduce your exposure to as many different kinds of potential toxins during your lifetime as possible. But don't drive yourself nuts over it. We are exposed to all kinds of toxins during our lives. Most health experts agree that the advantages of eating a diet rich in fruits and vegetables far outweigh the risks from consuming pesticide residues.

SAVE A BUNDLE BY BUYING LOCAL

While we're talking about the benefits of organics, let me point out a great way to get lots of fresh produce and still save money: buy fruits and vegetables in season directly from local farmers. Many towns and cities across the country are within easy distance of an organic farm, farmers' market, food-growing cooperative, or community supported agriculture (CSA) program. These are worthy institutions to support.

Most farms that welcome the public are open on Saturday mornings or even during weekdays. Or they may sell at local farmers' markets. Because small local farmers generally don't ship all over the country and are only growing food for local consumers, their produce will not be laden with the fungicides needed for similar food to arrive unblemished after long transport, such as from California to New York. Many local farms use organic growing practices even though they haven't received organic certification. Visit all the vendors at the farmers' market to make sure you are getting the best quality for the best price.

Some cities have nearby farms, mostly organic, that give consumers the option to order produce online every week. The farmer will typically designate delivery drop-off points where you can pick up the produce. Sometimes it will already be divided and waiting in a bin with your name on it. Other farmers deliver produce or dry goods in a truck that's met by customers who help unload it and divide up the contents.

Community-based farms are sprouting up all over the United States. Sometimes these farms are supported by local governments, but more often private nonprofit organizations run the day-to-day operations. The county employees I've met who organize or acquire land for the farms are often farsighted, dedicated leaders who say they would like to see every condominium, school, and shopping mall have a nearby food garden. Now that would be progress!

CSA farms have variable growing seasons. In my Florida CSA we have an average growing season of twenty-eight weeks, or about half the year. A membership, known

When Is Buying Organic a Priority?

Each year, the Environmental Working Group (EWG) publishes a list of the most-contaminated fruits and vegetables, in addition to a list of those that harbor the fewest pesticides. Use their list, which can be found at www.foodnews.org, as a guide when deciding whether buying organic is worth the price.

The "dirty dozen" are conventionally grown fruits and vegetables that have the most pesticides:

- celery
- peaches
- strawberries
- apples
- blueberries
- nectarines
- sweet bell peppers
- spinach
- cherries
- kale and collard greens
- potatoes
- grapes (imported)

These conventionally grown fruits and vegetables have the fewest pesticides:

- onions
- avocados
- sweet corn (frozen)
- pineapples
- mangoes
- sweet peas (frozen)
- asparagus
- kiwifruit
- cabbages
- eggplants

Do your best when deciding between organic and conventionally grown produce—and wash your fruits and veggies well before eating them. When you stop buying meat and dairy products, you can use some of the money you save to buy other organic foods, at least once in a while.

as a "share," costs about $450. That's about $16 a week for four to five grocery bags full of freshly picked, luscious vegetables and occasionally fruits. Prices vary at different CSAs around the country, but wherever you live, you would be hard-pressed to find anything close to the variety, quality, and quantity of vegetables that you get from a CSA for a similar price at your local market. In addition, you and your family can usually visit the farm that grows your food and have a direct relationship with the farmer. There is nothing quite like a child's wide-eyed expression when she digs in the dirt, harvests a potato for the first time, and realizes that food doesn't originate at a store!

Okay, now you have my pitch. Follow me, and I'll show you how to put my money-saving philosophy into practice.

CHAPTER 2

financial planning for food shopping

When you hear the term "financial planning," you think about retirement, right? But you can apply the principles of financial planning to food shopping. When you shop for groceries and prepare your meals, adopt some habits and strategies that will ensure you can achieve the financial goal of eating well on $4 a day per person. To make it easy for you to begin, I have developed some ground rules and tips for eating as healthfully—and inexpensively—as possible. Let's start with ways to put the ground rules into action:

9

Tweak Your Taste Buds

An effective strategy for fooling your taste buds is to eat the same types of foods you've always enjoyed but adjust the recipes to include less expensive (and more healthful) ingredients. Many of us grew up believing chicken soup was good for our souls, for chasing the flu, and for making strong bodies. A soup chock-full of beans and greens instead of chicken is just as comforting, while providing the protein and calcium you need at a lower price. If you use the right seasonings, you can re-create the savory richness of chicken in a beans-and-greens soup, without the expense. One ingredient that pumps up the flavor of soup without high cost is miso. A fermented paste made from soy (and sometimes other beans, rice, and barley), miso is high in protein and rich in vitamins and minerals.

Minestrone is a bean soup with pasta and a few veggies thrown in, and it often contains chicken broth. When you make it at home, replace the chicken broth with water mixed with several teaspoons of vegetable broth powder, and use whatever beans and whole-grain pasta are on sale or on hand. (One of the things I love about making minestrone is that it gives me an opportunity to use up all the "mature" vegetables in the fridge.)

Another great makeover candidate is chili. This classic stick-to-your-ribs stew is usually made with ground or cubed beef, but it can be just as spicy and satisfying—and a lot less expensive—if made with beans instead. However, if chili is just not chili in your book without a meaty texture and flavor, add textured soy protein (TSP), which can be found in most natural food stores.

1. Cook from scratch. Because convenience foods are more expensive than whole foods, one of the key ways to eat for less is to cook from scratch. This may seem like a daunting proposition if you're used to relying on processed packaged foods and takeout. But cooking from scratch doesn't have to be time-consuming or complicated, as you'll see from my recipes. If you prepare a few big batches of beans and whole grains once a week and store them in the refrigerator, you'll have the foundation for many quick meals throughout the week.

2. Eat a variety of beans, fruits, vegetables, and whole grains. A nutritious diet is based on a variety of fresh foods. Getting the recommended two servings of beans or legumes, three servings of fruits, four serving of vegetables, and five servings of whole grains every day may seem impossible if you are trying to squeeze them into the standard American diet. However, it's easy if you follow my recipes. Throughout this book you'll find a host of tips for buying fresh fruits and vegetables and other pantry staples inexpensively.

3. Be open to trying new foods and flavors. As you stop eating expensive, health-depleting meats and dairy products, you'll be replacing them with protein- and vitamin-rich plant-based foods that may be unfamiliar to you. Make it a goal to try one or two new foods each week. You'll find that your taste buds will become accustomed to purer, simpler flavors, and processed foods will lose their appeal.

Two items that will gobble up your food budget are snacks and desserts. Replacing high-priced candy bars, chips, cookies, and cupcakes with more sensible choices, such as fresh fruits, will save you money immediately. Not only are bananas easy to grab when you run out the door for the day, but they also win in the price department. A medium banana costs about $.20. Apples are also a terrific snack because they travel well, they're nutritious, and they're very easy on the budget.

Our mothers always said that eating an apple a day keeps the doctor away. Today, I say that apples keep away both the doctor *and* the repo man.

Other portable snacks are dried fruits and nuts. Combine the two with non-dairy chocolate chips and puffed-grain cereal to make your own trail mix for a fraction of what it costs ready-made.

Air-popped popcorn, flavored with your favorite seasonings at home, costs just pennies instead of the $7 or so you pay at a movie theater. Toss a few nondairy semisweet chocolate chips on top of hot popped corn, and you'll have a decadent, sweet-and-savory combo. In fact, just eating the chocolate chips alone is a guilty pleasure you can indulge in if you just have to have a sweet chocolate fix. In many stores you can find a twelve-ounce bag of these morsels on sale for $2. At thirty-two chips (and only seventy calories!) per serving, there are approximately twenty-three servings per bag. That's less than a dime per serving.

Finally, when it comes to snacking, think outside the box. Garbanzo beans or leftover brown rice mixed with salsa can be a quick, filling snack. If you don't have leftovers in the refrigerator to fall back on, try oatmeal. There's no rule that says oatmeal can be eaten only for breakfast. Many people don't realize that even long-cooking rolled oats can be softened and made ready to eat quickly. Simply pour boiling water over them and let them sit for ten minutes. Top the oatmeal with a sliced banana or some in-season blueberries or strawberries, and you'll have a nutritious, affordable snack that will hold you until the next meal. The cost is $.10 for the oatmeal and $.20 for the banana or $.31 for a small amount of berries. It doesn't get much cheaper than that, does it?

> ## How to Use Textured Soy Protein to Replace Meat
>
> Made from defatted soy flour that has been cooked under pressure, extruded into various shapes, and dried, textured soy protein (TSP) has a long shelf life if kept dry in tightly closed containers. It is an excellent, low-fat source of protein and fiber, and iron, magnesium, and other minerals and vitamins. Depending on the shape of the TSP, you can substitute it for ground meat or meat chunks in recipes. To use TSP, simply rehydrate it with hot water or vegetable broth, which will increase both its volume and weight. One ounce of dry TSP will replace approximately three ounces of meat and will cost about $.25 per serving.

ELLEN'S TOP TEN MONEY-SAVING TIPS

Here are ten money-saving tips I developed over years of thrifty shopping. These are the most effective ways I know to save money on food and get rock-bottom prices, week after week:

1. Use your head, not your heart (or stomach), when you shop. To avoid the urge to impulse shop, be smart and use a shopping list. During the week, as you run out of items, write down what you need on a running list—and stick to it!

Don't try to use shopping as therapy and buy expensive treats that give only fleeting happiness. To save money, you need to keep your emotions balanced—always remember to stick to your budget and that shopping list.

Never shop on an empty stomach. If you're starving, buy a banana or two and have a quick snack before walking down the aisles. You'll buy less if you're not feeling ravenous while you shop. The same idea applies to eating out. I usually keep a big bowl of cooked beans and brown rice in the refrigerator. If I'm going out to dinner, I'll heat some up with a little salsa for a quick snack just before I head out the door. This keeps me from ordering too many menu items, like expensive appetizers and side dishes, which can significantly add to the tab.

2. Check the unit prices. Most supermarkets show unit prices on their shelf labels, and checking unit prices is the fastest way I know to figure out if I'm getting a bargain. The unit price is almost always the price per ounce. It may seem basic, but when people are in a hurry to get their shopping over with, they just don't look at this information. You can find the unit price posted even in the refrigerated and frozen-foods sections. It is the lowest common denominator—the number you will use to compare every product against another size, brand, or type to determine which one is the best buy.

One word of caution: You can't compare dried beans to canned beans ounce for ounce. For example, the per-ounce price for canned beans may be $.05, the same as for dried beans. But an ounce of dried beans yields three to four ounces of cooked beans, making dried beans one-third to one-quarter the price of canned. Factor that in as you compare prices. That said, canned beans are still incredibly cheap relative to most other foods. If you need the convenience that canned beans offer, it is better to buy them than not eat beans at all.

3. Buy in bulk—within reason. Bigger usually means you're getting a better deal. Let's take dried beans as an example. An eight-pound bag of pinto beans will make more than one hundred half-cup servings of cooked beans. You can buy just such a bag at a big-box store for about $6. Do the math and you'll see that each serving costs just $.06. Be forewarned, however, that buying larger sizes is not always the most frugal option. For example, a bigger box of cereal may actually be more expensive than the smaller size, ounce per ounce. Always comparison shop (look at the unit price) and see if you are actually getting a better bargain.

The less time a company spends packaging and preparing a product for transport, the lower the cost of the item. If your local supermarket has a bulk-foods section, you can typically save money by buying food in bulk. You can portion out exactly how much you want, so you aren't forced to buy more than you need.

If you live alone or cook for just yourself, frozen produce may be a better choice than fresh. You can prepare the exact portion you want to eat and put the rest back in the freezer for another day, instead of risking that fresh produce will go bad before you get to it. A large bag of frozen blueberries can last a long time if you're using just a few in your morning oatmeal. On the other hand, with fresh berries it's tempting to eat most or all of your half-pint purchase in one sitting. So just watch yourself.

One good option is to stock up on fresh berries when they are in season and freeze them yourself. I've found, for example, that blueberries in season average about $2.50 per pound, or $.16 per ounce. A forty-eight-ounce bag of frozen blueberries can cost $12.99, or $.27 per ounce. So you can see that, when they cost $2.50 per pound, it's totally worth it to buy fresh blueberries. But, as always, it pays to do the math: when a pint of fresh blueberries costs more than $5, buying frozen is the better deal.

4. Shop the circumference of the store. The grocery store is organized to entice you to spend as much money as possible. Less profitable whole foods tend to be located around the circumference of the store (the exception is dry goods, such as beans and grains).

Don't purchase convenience foods, such as prewashed and cut vegetables or premade sandwiches. These boxed or bagged foods are more costly, and you are better off buying your own ingredients and doing the prep work yourself. You'll find the less-expensive alternatives in the produce, grain, and bean sections. Even some fairly simple "prepared" items cost too much. For instance, I love medjool dates, and for a treat I enjoy them rolled in shredded dried coconut. One local natural food store sells a package of twelve coconut-covered dates for $7.29, or about $.61 each. By buying the dates and coconut separately, I can make my own for a mere $.17 each.

5. Check the entire supermarket shelf—up, down, and all around. Since consumers tend to purchase items that are at eye level, the most expensive foods are often displayed at this height so they can be easily located. Look on the top and bottom shelves for better bargains. Competition is fierce for good placement on store shelves. Often, sale items are displayed at the front of the store or at the end of aisles. However, don't assume that items with these strategic placements are always a bargain. Product manufacturers or distributors may simply be paying the retailer for favorable display space.

6. Buy store brands when possible. In doing research for this book, I found that store-brand prices almost always beat brand-name prices, sometimes by a large amount. This is especially true for staples, such as dried beans, flour, grains, and salt. In addition, most major supermarket chains now offer their own brand of organic foods, which makes buying organic on a budget a lot easier.

7. Pay with cash. Using cash and carrying only the amount you intend to spend will keep you within your budget. It's that simple. This may mean going to the ATM once a month, putting aside grocery money in an envelope, and using only that cash for food. This method will guarantee that you won't buy more than you can afford.

Use a calculator at the grocery store and keep track of costs as you add items to your cart so you won't be caught short. If, despite your best calculations, your order total exceeds the amount of money you have, don't be afraid to hand a few things back to the cashier. Trust me—you won't be the first person (or the last) to do so.

8. Keep your receipts. If you discover that your store (or even another store) is running a sale on products you recently purchased at a higher price, you are entitled to go back to the store to ask for the lower price. I keep my recent receipts in the glove compartment in an envelope or in a separate part of my wallet. That way I always have them handy so I can dash into the store for a refund of the difference between what I paid and the sale price.

9. Track prices. Keep track of the prices of items you purchase often and make up a chart to carry with you when you shop. That way, if something is "on sale," you will know if you are really getting a better price. Here's a sample chart to help you keep track of items and costs:

GROCERY ITEM/SIZE	STORE 1	STORE 2	STORE 3
Dried pinto beans, eight-pound bag			

When you find a good price on a product, buy extra if it won't spoil. My treat is nondairy semisweet chocolate chips. When these morsels go on sale, I'm there, buying four bags at a time. To satisfy a sweet tooth, I'll eat a few small handfuls of chocolate chips instead of a less-healthful, higher-priced prepared baked good.

10. Buy local or grow your own. Don't be afraid to test your own green thumb. If you have no backyard, plant vegetables right alongside the flowers in your front yard. Plant them in containers on your balcony, patio, or porch. Perhaps a neighbor or friend without the time or the interest to tend her own garden would let you plant in her yard in exchange for some of the bounty. Finally, be sure to check out CSAs and farmers' markets (see pages 7 and 135).

OVERCOMING OBJECTIONS

Now that we've explored some ideas for how to implement your financial food plan, let's look at just a few of the most common objections that people come up with to avoid making the change—and how to overcome them:

Sprout the Perfect Indoor Garden

For fun and fabulous nutrition, grow your own sprouts. Sprouted seeds contain calcium, iron, magnesium, potassium, protein, and vitamins A, C, and E, just to name a few goodies. Sprouts also contain enzymes that aid digestion.

From a price perspective, sprouts are a tremendous value. Growing sprouts requires much less effort than planting traditional outdoor or window gardens. Rinsing and draining several different kinds of sprouts takes only about fifteen minutes a day and can provide a wide variety of fresh vegetables not available in markets—and all for just pennies per serving. (For detailed information on sprouting, or to purchase supplies, visit sproutpeople.org.)

1. Cooking from scratch takes too much time. My students often complain, "But I just don't have time to cook beans from scratch." Here's what I tell them: You can cook up a batch of beans in a couple of hours and eat them throughout the week. If you're home on Sunday evenings, put on a pot of beans. If you have a pressure cooker, get in the habit of cooking beans in it. Using a pressure cooker will cut the cooking time in half or more. When you let the pressure cooker do the work, it takes very little effort to cook dried beans.

Other foods can be prepared in advance as well. Take time once a week to prep vegetables that can be tossed into salads at the last minute. Cut-up veggies stored in a glass container in the refrigerator will keep for two to three days or even longer, depending on the vegetable.

2. Beans give me gas. Approximately 25 percent of people in the United States and other Western countries experience *dyspepsia*, a recurrent or persistent pain or discomfort that is primarily located in the upper abdomen. It can be caused by lactose intolerance or an inability to digest beans. Many people find that after about three weeks of eating beans every day, this problem wanes. If you're new to beans, start with smaller ones, such as lentils. Then work your way up to midsized and larger beans, such as garbanzos. Soaking dried beans, adding kombu to the cooking water, and cooking the beans until they are very soft and tender are three steps you can take to reduce any potential discomfort from eating beans.

3. Fruits and vegetables are boring. Excuse me? There are dozens and dozens of varieties of fruits and vegetables. If you don't like a few, exchange them for ones you do. Try new ones. You may surprise yourself. In my cooking classes, I always ask the students for a show of hands in response to this question: Who would like to be stranded on a deserted island with nothing but brussels sprouts to eat? Usually, about half the class, including me, raises their hands. We're the ones who don't have the supertaster gene. To those that do, green leafy vegetables taste bitter. If you have this gene, sprinkle some balsamic vinegar and a little soy sauce over the greens, and the bitterness should diminish. If you are ever again visited by the thought that fruits and vegetables don't offer enough variety, try counting the types of animals in the meat department—not so many.

4. I'm the only one in my family eating this way. Being the only vegan in the family can be challenging, for sure. But often people find that when they start enjoying terrific health and go through life-changing transformations in terms of their weight, appearance, and attitude, family members not only become supportive but often want a piece of the action too. So carry on, knowing that as a result of your exemplary behavior, you will be a role model for others.

If you must prepare separate meals, make sure you eat a healthful snack before making foods that are not on your plan. Keep your food in separate parts of the pantry or kitchen so you aren't tempted by items you don't want to eat. Make sure that if a family member is eating your favorite brand of chocolate chip cookie, you have an alternative food you can turn to. Don't let temptation stare you in the face and call your name!

It is always much easier to live with someone who eats the way you do. However, people change and grow in different directions throughout their lifetimes. For many, it is more important to have a loving and respectful life partner than to sit with a clone at the dinner table. You will have to find ways of coping and managing if your partner, or any other member of your family, does not join you on this journey. You can still accomplish your goals of saving money and eating well, whether you are on your own or your entire family joins you in your mission.

CHAPTER 3

plant-based nutrition and cooking 101

You may wonder if you'll get enough protein and calcium if you give up meat and dairy products. Much research has been done to prove that you can get more than adequate and absorbable supplies of protein and calcium by eating a vegan diet based on the four food groups. Popular books such as *Prevent and Reverse Heart Disease* by Caldwell Esselstyn, MD; *Program for Reversing Diabetes* and *Turn Off the Fat Genes* by Neal Barnard, MD; and *The China Study* by T. Colin Campbell, PhD, include some of the most current research and information about the immediate, long-lasting, and positive effects of plant-based diets.

Count on the Four Food Groups

FRUITS: 3 or more servings per day

Fruits are rich in beta-carotene, fiber, and vitamin C. Include at least one serving each day of fruits that are high in vitamin C—citrus fruits, melons, and strawberries are all good choices. Choose whole fruits over fruit juices, which do not contain very much fiber.

Serving size: 1 medium piece of fruit • ½ cup cooked fruit • 4 ounces juice

VEGETABLES: 4 or more servings per day

Vegetables are packed with nutrients; they provide beta-carotene, calcium, fiber, iron, riboflavin, and vitamin C, to name a few. Dark green leafy vegetables, such as broccoli, cabbage, chicory, collards, kale, and mustard and turnip greens, are especially good sources of these important nutrients. Dark yellow and orange vegetables, such as carrots, pumpkins, sweet potatoes, and winter squash, provide extra beta-carotene. Include generous portions of a variety of vegetables in your diet.

Serving size: 1 cup raw vegetables • ½ cup cooked vegetables

LEGUMES: 2 or more servings per day

Legumes—which is another name for beans, lentils, and peas—are good sources of B vitamins, calcium, fiber, iron, protein, and zinc. This group also includes baked beans, garbanzo beans, refried beans, soymilk, tempeh, and textured soy protein.

Serving size: ½ cup cooked beans • 4 ounces tofu or tempeh • 8 ounces soymilk

WHOLE GRAINS: 5 or more servings per day

Grains are rich in fiber and other complex carbohydrates, in addition to B vitamins, protein, and zinc. This group includes barley, bulgur, brown rice, corn, millet, whole-grain pasta, hot or cold whole-grain cereal, and whole-grain bread or tortillas. Build each of your meals around hearty whole grains.

Serving size: ½ cup rice or other grain • 1 ounce dry cereal • 1 slice bread

As long as you eat a varied diet from all four food groups (see box above), in the quantities suggested, you won't be hungry, you will feel very satisfied, and you won't need to worry about counting another calorie again (if maintaining a healthy weight is a priority for you too). Some people might consider a diet based on beans and grains to be spartan, but many cultures have developed richly flavored, delicious cuisines using these foods. Think of black beans and rice with fresh salsa and avocado, savory Indian curries, Greek salads, and Chinese stir-fries. I rely on beans and grains in many of my recipes. You'll find that these foods are incredibly satisfying—but not at the expense of your pocketbook.

A good way to ensure that your diet is well-rounded and rich in nutrients is to get the recommended number of servings from the four food groups (see box above). Simply combine a variety of breakfast, lunch, snack, and dinner recipes from this book to meet those requirements. The only essential nutrient your diet will be lacking is vitamin B_{12}, which used to be found in our soil and on vegetables. But since we now clean vegetables so thoroughly, vitamin B_{12} must be obtained in individual or multivitamin supplements or through enriched products, such as some soymilks and cereals.

BEANS 101

If you're unfamiliar with cooking beans from scratch, it's easier than you might think, and it will have a dramatic and positive effect on your food budget. One of my top cost-cutting secrets is buying dried pinto beans in bulk at big-box stores. These beans cost a little less than other dried beans. If you stock up by purchasing the largest bag of pinto beans you can find, four ounces of cooked beans will cost you a dime. Another secret to eating on a budget is simply getting your main protein from beans or a bean product, adding whole grains, keeping the main portion of your meal centered on vegetables, and having fruit for dessert. And eating lots of salad. When you eat this way, salads will not break the bank—and you'll feel *so* good, financially and physically.

Your first step to eating better for less is to buy a large bag of dried beans. To get delicious cooked beans every time, follow the directions in the sidebar "Six Steps to Great Beans." Refer to table 2 (page 21) for cooking times for specific beans.

Soaking dried beans before cooking can enhance their tenderness and flavor. Soaking may also help minimize the gas that some people experience when they first start eating beans. When you eat beans often, your body will adapt and digest them more easily. Some people find that small beans are easier to digest than large ones. To start, try eating small amounts of black beans, black-eyed peas, and lentils. After you are accustomed to eating smaller beans, try larger beans, such as garbanzo and pinto beans. Adding kombu (a type of sea vegetable) at the beginning of the cooking process may help minimize gas while adding flavor and nutrients. You can also just try cooking the beans ten to fifteen minutes longer than stated in the directions.

Most dried beans require a ratio of one part beans to three parts water for cooking. Garbanzo beans and soybeans, because they are larger and more dense, take a 1:4 ratio of beans to water. Lentils, because they are smaller than the average bean, take a 1:2 ratio of beans

Six Steps to Great Beans

1. Examine the dried beans and throw away any foreign particles or beans that are discolored or shriveled.

2. Rinse the beans with water and drain.

3. Soak the beans for eight to twelve hours (at room temperature or in the refrigerator) before cooking. Some small beans do not require soaking.

4. Put the beans in a large pot and cover with fresh water. Bring to a boil over medium-high heat, then decrease the heat to low and keep the pot covered while the beans are cooking. Add more water, if necessary, during cooking so the beans remain covered with water.

5. Add seasonings to the beans while they cook. Many people believe that the taste of beans improves with salt, but others believe that adding salt can extend the cooking time and possibly toughen the beans.

6. When the beans are tender but firm, they're ready to eat or add to your favorite recipes.

to water. In fact, because this is the same ratio used to cook brown rice and many other whole grains, some people like to cook lentils and grains together to save preparation and cleanup time.

Lentils and split peas are so small that they don't need to be soaked. Other beans need to be soaked for eight to twelve hours. This can be done overnight, while you are sleeping, or while you are at work. Simply soak the beans in the appropriate amount of water (see the ratios listed above), making sure that the beans are covered by at least one inch of water. After the beans have soaked, drain the water and replace it with fresh water.

Alternatively, if you prefer a shortcut over a long soak, put the beans and water in a large saucepan and bring to a boil over medium-high heat. Boil the beans for one minute, remove the pan from the heat, and let the beans soak for one hour. Drain the beans, return them to the pan, and cover them with fresh water. Cover the pan, bring the beans to a gentle boil over medium-high heat, then decrease the heat to low and simmer the beans. Depending on the size of the beans, they should be tender after one and one-half to two hours. Taste one or two beans to be sure. If they aren't quite done, continue cooking until tender. For the best results, test the beans frequently. Add hot water, if necessary, to keep the beans covered with liquid.

Cooking beans in a pressure cooker cuts the cooking time down to literally just a few minutes, so you may want to consider investing in one; the cost will eventually be offset by a reduction in your utility bill. As an added benefit, pressure-cooked beans are easier and more convenient to prepare, so you may be more likely to eat them. Some beans require soaking before pressure cooking, but if you don't have time to do that (or if you forget), you can simply cook the beans under pressure several minutes longer. A few bean varieties, such as split peas, should not be cooked in a pressure cooker because they fall apart too easily or foam excessively, which can clog the pressure-release valve. Never fill a pressure cooker more than halfway with beans and water.

Table 2 (page 21) is a guide to help you cook beans, either in a saucepan or a pressure cooker. The times are for soaked beans (except where indicated). For pressure-cooked beans, the cooking time is for beans cooked under high pressure (fifteen pounds) and includes allowing the pressure to come down naturally. If you use a quick-release method instead, you will need to cook the beans a few minutes longer.

Slow Cooking

The Foolproof Way to Cook Beans: A convenient and easy method for cooking dried beans is to use a slow cooker. Simply soak the beans in water for eight to twelve hours overnight. In the morning, drain the beans, put them in the slow cooker, cover them with fresh water, and set the slow cooker on low. Then go off to work and let the beans cook all day. Larger beans in particular can cook on low heat for eight hours or even longer if you are working late. Slow cookers, even programmable models with timers, are inexpensive, widely available, and can easily last twenty years or longer. If you don't already own a slow cooker, consider buying one. It would definitely be a good investment.

Cooking times for dried beans				TABLE 2
BEANS, SOAKED (1 CUP DRIED)	WATER IN CUPS	STOVETOP COOKING TIMES	PRESSURE COOKING TIMES (AT HIGH PRESSURE)	YIELD IN CUPS
black (turtle) beans	3	1 to 1½ hours	5 to 8 minutes	2
black-eyed peas	3	1 to 1½ hours	10 to 11 minutes (don't soak)	2¼
cannellini beans	3	1 to 1½ hours	5 to 8 minutes	2
garbanzo beans (chickpeas)	3	1 to 1½ hours	8 to 13 minutes	2½
great northern beans	3	1 to 1½ hours	5 to 8 minutes	2¼
lentils, brown	2	30 to 40 minutes	8 to 10 minutes (don't soak)	2
lentils, red	2	30 to 40 minutes	4 to 6 minutes (don't soak)	2
navy or small white beans	3	1 to 1½ hours	5 to 8 minutes	2
pinto beans	3	1 to 1½ hours	5 to 7 minutes	2¼
red kidney beans	3	1 to 1½ hours	5 to 8 minutes	2
split peas, green or yellow	3	30 to 45 minutes	not recommended	2

NOTE: At higher altitudes, dried beans take more time to rehydrate and cook. The difference begins to be noticeable above 3,500 feet. A pressure cooker can be useful at high altitudes, but you'll have to experiment with the cooking times. Begin by doubling the pressure-cooking times called for in table 2.

GRAINS 101

Cooking whole grains is quite easy. Just measure the grain and water into a saucepan according to the information in table 3 (page 22). (If you are cooking one cup of grain, use a two-quart saucepan.) Cover the saucepan and bring to a boil over high heat. Decrease the heat to low and steam the grain for the recommended cooking time. Lift the lid and test for tenderness. If the grain isn't tender, cover the saucepan and steam for five to ten minutes longer. If the grain needs more cooking time and all the water has been absorbed, add up to one-quarter cup of water, cover, and continue cooking. When the grain is tender, remove the saucepan from the heat and let the grain rest, covered, for five to ten minutes. Fluff with a fork just before serving.

Buckwheat is the exception to these basic directions. Because the grain is so porous and absorbs water quickly, it is best to bring the water to a boil first and then add the buckwheat. When the water returns to a boil, cover the saucepan, decrease the heat to low, and time the cooking from this point. For other useful hints about cooking grains, see "Tips for Preparing Great Grains" (page 23).

TABLE	3	Stovetop cooking times and yields for whole grains		
GRAIN (1 CUP DRY)	**WATER IN CUPS**	**COOKING TIMES**	**YIELD IN CUPS**	
amaranth	2½	20 to 25 minutes	2½	
barley, pearl	3	50 to 60 minutes	3½	
barley flakes	2	30 to 40 minutes	2½	
buckwheat groats	2	15 minutes	2½	
bulgur	2	15 minutes	2½	
cornmeal, fine grind	4	8 to 10 minutes	2½	
cornmeal, coarse grind	4	20 to 25 minutes	2½	
couscous	1	5 minutes	2	
millet, hulled	3 to 4	20 to 25 minutes	3½	
oats, rolled	2½	5 minutes	2	
oats, steel-cut	3	15 to 20 minutes	3½	
quinoa	2	15 to 20 minutes	2¾	
rice, brown basmati	2½	35 to 40 minutes	3	
rice, long-grain brown	2½	45 to 55 minutes	3	
rice, short-grain brown	2 to 2½	45 to 55 minutes	3	
rice, quick-cooking brown	1¼	10 minutes	2	
rice, wild	3	50 to 60 minutes	4	
rye berries	3 to 4	1 hour	3	
rye flakes	2	10 to 15 minutes	3	
spelt berries	3 to 4	40 to 50 minutes	2½	
teff	3	5 to 20 minutes	3½	
triticale berries	3	1 hour and 45 minutes	2½	
wheat, cracked	2	20 to 25 minutes	2¼	
wheat berries	3	2 hours	2½	

TABLE 4

Pressure-cooking times and yields for whole grains

GRAIN (1 CUP DRY)	WATER IN CUPS	MINUTES UNDER HIGH PRESSURE*	YIELD IN CUPS
amaranth	1½	4	2½
barley, pearl	4	15 to 20	3½
buckwheat groats	1¾	3	2½
bulgur	1½	5 to 8	2½
kamut berries	3	35 to 40	2¾
millet	2	10	3½ to 4
oats, quick-cooking rolled	1⅔	6	2
oats, steel-cut	1⅔	11	3½
quinoa	2	1 to 2	2¾
rice, basmati	1½	5 to 7	3
rice, brown	1½	20 to 40	3
rice, wild	3	22 to 25	4
spelt berries	3	35 to 45	2½
triticale	3	40	2½
wheat berries	3	35 to 45	2½

* Remove from the heat and allow the pressure to come down naturally for about ten minutes after cooking.

Tips for Preparing Great Grains

- Flattened or rolled grain flakes, such as barley, rye, triticale, and wheat, do not need to be cooked when added to cold cereals. They add crunchiness and will soften a bit when served with nondairy milk, such as almond milk, rice milk, or soymilk.

- If you prefer whole grains with a crunchier texture, cook the grains using a ratio of one part grains to two parts water.

- Buckwheat groats are available toasted and untoasted. Cooking times are the same.

- Short-grain brown rice is sometimes labeled "sweet," "glutinous," or "sticky."

- Bulgur can be covered with one inch of warm water and soaked for one hour to soften. It is then ready to use in salads, such as Tabouli (page 58).

- Quinoa should be put into a fine-mesh strainer and rinsed well for one to two minutes to remove the natural saponin layer, a harmless, protective coating that will impart a bitter flavor if not rinsed off. Some quinoa is available prewashed and does not need to be rinsed.

- Teff can be eaten raw or cooked. Sprinkle raw teff on salads or over cooked cereals to increase your nutrient and fiber intake.

STOCKING YOUR PANTRY

By now you understand that the key to eating well on $4 a day is eating more beans, grains, and greens. These will be the staples of your kitchen. Fortunately for you, some of the most nutritious foods cost the least, so you can afford to stock up. Where to start? You'll find that you're more likely to cook healthful, low-cost meals if you have the basic ingredients on hand, so begin with a good variety of dried beans and whole grains—six to twelve different types. To protect your investment, store these foods in airtight glass jars (plastic containers can be made with toxic ingredients that increase health risks, so I recommend using glass). Mason jars with either screw-top or wire-clamp lids work well. Reusing pasta sauce jars is an even less-expensive option. Properly stored, whole grains will keep for several months, and beans will keep even longer.

You'll also want to have a variety of dried herbs and spices at your disposal. To pay the least for these items, buy only what you can use in a few months. When you buy these items in the bulk-foods section of your natural food store (or a better-stocked supermarket), you can scoop out just the amount of herbs and spices you need, for a fraction of what it costs to buy them by the jar. Buy a single bay leaf, if that's all you need. Ethnic markets are another great source for herbs and spices (and for staples such as rice and sea vegetables). Buy one-hundred-gram packets and store them in glass jars. Save and reuse old spice bottles or jelly jars to store your dried herbs and spices.

If you haven't stocked your pantry this way in the past, at first you may find yourself spending more on certain items, such as high-quality oils and vinegars, miso, tahini, and sea vegetables, which can come with substantial price tags. But your initial investment will pay off over time in several ways. Most of these ingredients last a long time; miso, for example, keeps indefinitely in the refrigerator. Most are used in small amounts, so that the actual cost per use is quite modest. Small amounts of potently flavored condiments, such as balsamic vinegar, make a big impact in a recipe and will give you quite a bang for your buck.

Keep in mind that the following ingredients will keep for months in a cool, dry place or in the refrigerator: cocoa powder; dates (refrigerated); nondairy chocolate chips; nuts and seeds (refrigerated or frozen); nut and seed butters (refrigerated); nut and seed oils, such as sesame oil (refrigerated); tempeh (refrigerated); whole-grain flours (refrigerated or frozen); and vinegars. Other higher-priced ingredients, such as vegan cheese, cream cheese, and sour cream, will keep for several weeks if properly wrapped and stored in the refrigerator; vegan nonhydrogenated margarine will keep for months in the refrigerator. Don't forget to check expiration dates when buying these items.

In order not to blow your budget at once, buy just one or two higher-priced ingredients each month and try out the recipes that use them. For example, try Tasty Tacos (page 92) and Load-'Em-Up Burritos (page 91), which both use avocados, on consecutive days. Avocados can cost more than a dollar each.

Follow the same principle when buying fresh herbs. There's no denying that fresh herbs can be pricey, and, unlike their dried counterparts, they have a fairly limited shelf life. So if you're buying fresh basil for one recipe, see what else you can prepare to use it up. (Of course, if you make a recipe and love it, there's no reason you can't make it again a few days later.)

Be sure to store fresh herbs properly. If they are bound by a rubber band, remove it. Put the herbs on a paper towel to absorb excess moisture and then seal the herbs (still wrapped in the paper towel) in a plastic bag. A better and less-expensive alternative to buying fresh herbs is to grow your own, either in a garden or on your windowsill, so you can pinch off leaves as you need them. Many grocery stores sell fresh basil plants. After you use the basil leaves in a few recipes, find a sunny spot for the plant in your garden or in a pot near a window; it will keep producing new shoots and leaves.

> ### Frequently Used Herbs and Spices
>
> If you are basing your herb and spice purchases on the recipes in this book, the most commonly used varieties are basil, bay leaf, cilantro, cumin, curry powder, garlic, and parsley. Used less often are coriander, dill, dried onions, mint, oregano, rosemary, sage, and thyme.

WEEKLY MENU PLAN

To show how you can eat for very little money every day, I've created a $4-a-day menu plan for seven days. (In fact, one daily menu plan comes in under $3!) The menu plan uses recipes that can be found in this book and covers all the nutritional bases, including servings of protein, fruits or vegetables, and a whole grain at most meals. You can always add more beans, grains, or greens if you want to increase your intake of calories or other nutrients, and you don't have to squeeze all your daily requirements in at every meal. For example, if you eat beans at one meal, you don't have to combine them with grain to get a complete protein immediately. Eating whole grains later in the day works just as well.

I created a database of typical food prices by tracking and comparing prices between big-box stores and online stores over time. Generally, my database prices reflect the lowest average cost for products that can be found at these outlets. I did my shopping at several big-box stores, figuring that most readers will have access to similar stores. Often, prices at these stores were lower than those at grocery stores, but not always. My premise that you can eat well on $4 a day is based on pricing that's as accurate as I can calculate. However, food pricing can be volatile, and tomorrow's prices may differ from today's.

Food prices will also vary in different regions and at different times of the year, of course. I've based produce prices on in-season costs. Your costs may be less if you grow your own produce or take advantage of low prices from a nearby community garden or farmers' market. The point here is to show that you don't have to sacrifice your budget to eat healthfully.

To make it easier for you to add up the cost of several recipes when planning menus, the recipes on the following pages list the estimated cost for a single serving, rounded up to the closest $.25. (Recipes that cost less than $.25 are literally just a few pennies per serving, so these costs are excluded from the menu totals.)

Day One total = $2.25

BREAKFAST: Hot Whole-Grain Cereal (page 30) [less than $.25]

LUNCH: Hummus (page 103) [$.75] served with lettuce in whole wheat pita bread [less than $.25]

DINNER: Beans-and-Greens Stir-Fry (page 79) [$.75], served with ½ cup brown rice [less than $.25]

DESSERT/SNACK: On-the-Go Fruit Smoothie (page 123) [$.75]

Day Two total = $4.00

BREAKFAST: Breakfast Scramble (page 36) [$.50] served on a whole-grain flour tortilla [$.50]

LUNCH: Tasty Tacos (page 92) [$.25]

DINNER: Stone-Broke Soup (page 47) [$.50], served with beans [less than $.25]; Braised Collards or Kale (page 107) [$.25]

DESSERT/SNACK: Apple Crisp (page 114) [$1.00]

Day Three total = $4.00

BREAKFAST: Chorizo-Flavored Scramble (page 37) [$.75]

LUNCH: Delectable Lentil Soup (page 45) [$.50], served with ½ cup brown rice [less than $.25]

DINNER: Quesadillas with Not-So-Refried Beans (page 93) [$2.00]; Polenta (page 110) [less than $.25]

DESSERT/SNACK: Berries, Bananas, and More Smoothie (page 126) [$.75]

Day Four total = $4.00

BREAKFAST: Multigrain Cereal Combo (page 33) [$.50]

LUNCH: Portobello Poor Boy Sandwich (page 89) [**$2.00**]

DINNER: Penny-Pincher Pitas (page 88) [**$1.00**]

DESSERT/SNACK: Heavenly Mango Smoothie (page 125) [$.50]

Day Five total = $3.75

BREAKFAST: Millet Crunch (page 32) [$.75]

LUNCH: Easy Bean Salad (page 54) [$.75]

DINNER: Royal Stir-Fry (page 80) [**$1.00**]

DESSERT/SNACK: Coconut "Ice Cream" (page 122) [**$1.25**]

Day Six total = $4.00

BREAKFAST: Kid-Friendly Cocoa Puffs (page 34) [**$1.00**]

LUNCH: Working Lunch Salad and Dressing (page 59) [$.75], rolled in a whole-grain flour tortilla [$.25]

DINNER: Cuban Black Bean Soup (page 43) [$.50], served with ½ cup brown rice [**less than $.25**]; Wok-Sautéed Greens (page 106) [**$1.00**]

DESSERT/SNACK: ½ cup blueberries or strawberries [$.50]

Day Seven total = $3.75

BREAKFAST: Hot Wheat Cereal with Dates (page 31) [$.50]

LUNCH: Billfold-Saver Black Bean Burger (page 85) [$.50], served on a whole wheat bun or whole-grain bread [**less than $.25**]; Tropical Salad (page 57) [**$1.25**]

DINNER: Minestrone with Pasta Shells (page 44) [**$1.00**]

DESSERT/SNACK: Chocolate Mousse (page 121) [$.50]

TAKING THE PLUNGE

T o eat satisfying, healthful meals for the long term, depend on a variety of whole foods. Keep processed foods at the bottom of your shopping list if saving money is your number-one priority. To save money and cover the basic plant-based food groups, stick to buying foods in their most natural state. If your goal is to eat a well-balanced diet on as little money as possible, eat a simple variety of two or more servings of beans, five or more servings of whole grains, four or more servings of vegetables, and two to three fruits a day. You do not need complicated recipes, a shelf full of spices, or exotic ingredients to do this. A plum or apple can be dessert. Brown rice flavored with cinnamon and raisins can be a side dish, black beans with tomatoes and onions can be a main dish, and a simple salad of lettuce greens with three or four veggie toppings can meet your vegetable requirements for the day.

Although using recipes can certainly help you to vary your repertoire (not to mention help you show friends and families that eating vegan meals means eating great-tasting food), you also can plan out your daily and weekly menus quite easily by just sticking to the basics. Plant-based eating can be as simple or as complicated as you like. But most of all, it can be totally affordable, if you plan ahead and plan well.

You can see how easy it is to get expensive meat and junk food out of your kitchen and replace them with less costly, more nutritious alternatives. You are sure to get all kinds of ideas as you go along—and you'll be amazed at how much money you will save and how much better you will feel.

Whether you take the plunge and commit to eating this way full time or just substitute recipes in this book for a few high-priced meals each week is up to you. Many of the people I've taught said they find it easier to take the full plunge than to take baby steps. They love the feeling of cleansing their bodies and taste buds and find it more satisfying to develop an entirely new routine than to take a piecemeal approach. But by all means, choose whichever route works best for you. The fact is, once you discover how delicious plant-based whole foods really are, and find out how good you feel when you stop eating animal-based products, you may find yourself more motivated than you could have ever imagined. With my recipe tips, you will be able to unclog your budget and your arteries. It doesn't get much better than that.

I ask only one thing in return. Promise me that the next time you see a news story about how people on tight budgets can only afford processed or fast foods, you will contact the station and let them know how wrong they are. Tell them, "*Au contraire!* Let me show you a different way."

bolster
your budget
breakfasts

hot whole-grain CEREAL

Many people are familiar with rolled oats but may not be aware that other grains, such as barley, rye, triticale, and wheat, are also available in an easy-to-cook form. These rolled grains cook in just a few minutes. Or, if you are in a rush, put the grains in a cereal bowl with boiling water, cover the bowl, and allow the grains to sit for at least ten minutes.

2 cups water

1 cup rolled or steel-cut oats or rolled barley, rye, triticale, or wheat

1 teaspoon salt (optional)

Put the water in a 2-quart saucepan and bring to a boil over high heat. Stir in the oats and optional salt, decrease the heat to low, cover loosely, and cook for 20 to 30 minutes, or until the oats are soft and the water has been absorbed. Remove from the heat and let sit, covered, for 5 minutes before serving.

TIPS

- Before serving, top the cereal with berries or sliced fruit, chopped nuts, seeds, or a teaspoon of maple syrup.

- Adding berries is a good way to stretch your food budget, as just a few berries deliver a lot of flavor. Frozen berries are slightly cheaper per serving than fresh berries during the off-season.

- If using frozen fruit, allow it to defrost at room temperature for 30 minutes before adding it to the cereal, unless you enjoy a cold crunch with your warm cereal.

- Rather than spend money on premixed whole-grain cereals, make your own cereal blend by purchasing individual bags of your favorite grains and combining them yourself.

HOT *wheat cereal with dates*

MAKES 4 SERVINGS **$.50** PER SERVING

Hot cereal is the ultimate comfort food. This recipe showcases bulgur, a grain you might not associate with breakfast. You can also serve this as a side dish to complement a Middle Eastern or Indian meal.

> **2 cups water**
>
> **1 cup medium-grind bulgur**
>
> **⅔ cup chopped dates**
>
> **Pinch salt**
>
> **½ teaspoon vanilla extract**
>
> **¼ teaspoon ground cardamom**
>
> **¼ teaspoon ground nutmeg**
>
> **Plain or vanilla soymilk or rice milk** (optional)

Put the water, bulgur, dates, and salt in a medium saucepan and bring to a boil over medium-high heat, stirring constantly. Decrease the heat to low, cover, and cook, stirring occasionally, for 20 to 30 minutes, or until the bulgur is very tender. Remove from the heat and stir in the vanilla extract, cardamom, and nutmeg. Serve plain or with soymilk, if desired.

MILLET *crunch*

$.75 PER SERVING · **MAKES 1 SERVING**

Millet is one of the sweetest, most flavorful whole grains. The addition of nuts and fruit makes millet perfect for breakfast.

½ cup water

¼ cup millet

1 tablespoon sliced almonds

1 tablespoon chopped walnuts

4 strawberries, sliced (optional)

2 tablespoons raisins (optional)

Put the water in a small saucepan and bring to a boil over high heat. Stir in the millet, decrease the heat to low, cover, and cook for 20 minutes, or until all the water has been absorbed. Transfer to a cereal bowl and top with the almonds, walnuts, and optional strawberries and raisins. Serve hot.

TIPS

- Millet is naturally sweet, and adding fruit makes this cereal even sweeter. For additional sweetness, add agave nectar, maple syrup, or stevia. Go easy on the stevia—a little goes a very long way.

- If you don't use nuts in this recipe, the cost per serving drops to less than $.25. However, the protein and other nutrients they contain make nuts worth the extra expense.

- Any whole grain or combination of grains, such as barley, buckwheat, kamut, oats, spelt, teff, or triticale, can be substituted for the millet. See the cooking instructions for whole grains on pages 22 to 23.

multigrain cereal COMBO

MAKES 1 SERVING
$.50 PER SERVING

For decades, puffed corn, rice, and wheat have been used in commercial cereals, which usually contain excessive amounts of sugar and may even be "enhanced" with glow-in-the-dark colors to appeal to children. In their natural state, puffed grains are quite tasty. If you want some extra sweetness, just add fruit.

½ cup puffed corn, kamut, millet, rice, or wheat, or a combination

½ cup soymilk, almond milk, or oat milk

1 small banana, sliced, or ¼ cup berries in season (optional)

¼ cup chopped almonds

¼ cup chopped walnuts

Put one or more of the puffed grains in a cereal bowl and pour the soymilk on top. Add the optional banana and the almonds and walnuts. Serve immediately.

TIPS

- To avoid having many opened bags of whole grains in your pantry, combine the contents of several bags in one airtight container or store a quantity in the freezer.

- Puffed grains can also be combined with rolled or flaked grains, such as rolled oats or barley, rye, triticale, or wheat flakes. The variety is endless!

kid-friendly COCOA PUFFS

$1.00 PER SERVING   **MAKES 1 SERVING**

25¢ 25¢ 25¢ 25¢

This recipe is a more nutritious version of the classic kids' breakfast favorite. It contains no added sugar, but the banana and soymilk will give your child (and you!) a sweet start to the morning.

½ cup puffed corn

½ cup vanilla soymilk

1 teaspoon unsweetened cocoa powder

1 banana, sliced

Put the cereal in a bowl and pour the soymilk on top. Sprinkle with the cocoa powder and top with the banana. Serve immediately.

TIP: Since cocoa powder contains a small amount of caffeine, you may want to use less when making this cereal for young children. Many chocolate cereals do not contain real chocolate but use chocolate flavoring instead.

sweet potato MUFFINS

MAKES 10 MUFFINS   **$.50** PER SERVING

A cancer survivor in my cooking class served these muffins to her church congregation of 150. She reported to me with a chuckle: "The whole church loved the muffins and no one knew they were vegan!"

2 cups all-purpose whole wheat flour or whole wheat pastry flour

½ **cup sugar**

1 tablespoon baking powder

½ **teaspoon baking soda**

½ **teaspoon ground cinnamon**

½ **teaspoon salt**

¼ **teaspoon ground nutmeg**

1¾ cups mashed cooked sweet potatoes, or 1 can (15 ounces) **sweet potatoes, drained and mashed**

½ **cup raisins**

½ **cup water**

Preheat the oven to 375 degrees F.

Put the flour, sugar, baking powder, baking soda, cinnamon, salt, and nutmeg in a large bowl and stir to combine. Add the sweet potatoes, raisins, and water and stir until well combined.

Lightly coat ten muffin cups of a standard muffin tin with nonstick cooking spray. Fill each muffin cup almost to the top with batter. Bake for 25 to 30 minutes, until the tops of the muffins bounce back when pressed lightly and a toothpick inserted in the center of a muffin comes out clean. Let the muffins cool in the tin for 1 to 2 minutes before removing. Transfer to a rack to finish cooling. Serve warm or at room temperature.

TIP: Store leftover muffins in an airtight container in the refrigerator.

BREAKFAST *scramble*

$.50 PER SERVING   **MAKES 4 SERVINGS**

When I make this recipe for children's cooking classes, I start by saying, "Now for our magic show." Even adults ooh and aah when I transform stark white tofu into a beautiful omelet-colored dish. The anti-inflammatory spice turmeric provides the magic.

½ **cup water**

1 small onion, chopped

2 garlic cloves, minced

½ **green bell pepper, chopped**

¼ **red bell pepper, chopped**

1 package (14 ounces) **firm or extra-firm tofu, drained, and crumbled**

1 teaspoon chopped fresh parsley

½ **teaspoon ground turmeric**

Salt

Ground pepper

Put 2 tablespoons of the water, the onion, and garlic in a large nonstick skillet over medium heat and cook, stirring occasionally, for about 5 minutes, or until the onion is translucent, adding more water, 1 tablespoon at a time, as it evaporates. Add the green and red bell peppers and 1 to 2 more tablespoons of the water and continue to cook and stir until the vegetables are soft. Add the tofu, parsley, and turmeric and season with salt and pepper to taste. Stir until all the ingredients are well combined. Cook for about 5 more minutes, until the scramble is hot and steaming.

TIP: To make a breakfast burrito, use the scramble as a filling for a corn or whole-grain flour tortilla. Warm the tortilla until pliable. Spoon the scramble onto the tortilla and roll it up burrito style.

chorizo-flavored SCRAMBLE

MAKES 10 SERVINGS **$.75** PER SERVING

For those who enjoy a south-of-the-border flavor, here's a breakfast scramble without the cholesterol. Serving the scramble in a tortilla will add even more south-of-the-border flair.

3 slices vegan bacon

3 tablespoons water, or 1 tablespoon olive oil

¼ cup finely chopped onion

4 to 6 garlic cloves, minced

1 package (12 ounces) **vegan burger crumbles**

1 package (14 ounces) **firm tofu, drained and crumbled**

2 tablespoons cider vinegar

2 tablespoons raisins, soaked in water for 10 minutes and drained

1 to 3 small hot dried red chiles, crushed (optional)

2 teaspoons low-sodium soy sauce

1 teaspoon agave nectar or maple syrup

1 teaspoon dried oregano

¼ teaspoon chili powder

¼ teaspoon ground black pepper

¼ teaspoon ground cumin

¼ teaspoon ground turmeric

Salt

10 (6-inch) **corn tortillas or whole-grain flour tortillas, warmed** (optional)

Mist a small skillet with nonstick cooking spray. Put the vegan bacon in the skillet and cook over medium heat until crispy, for about 10 minutes, flipping the slices so that they cook evenly on both sides. Remove the slices from the skillet and transfer them to a plate to cool. When cool enough to handle, crumble them into small pieces.

Put the water, onion, and garlic in a large nonstick skillet over medium-high heat and cook and stir for about 5 minutes, or until the onion is soft. Add the vegan burger crumbles, tofu, vinegar, raisins, optional chiles, soy sauce, agave nectar, oregano, chili powder, pepper, cumin, and turmeric. Stir until evenly distributed. Cook and stir for about 5 minutes, or until heated through. Add the crumbled vegan bacon and salt to taste. Stir until well incorporated. Serve immediately, with the optional tortillas, if desired.

save your loot
soups

SIMPLE *blender soup*

$.75 PER SERVING   **MAKES 2 SERVINGS**

In our dreams, many of us are gourmet cooks. However, in reality—especially at six o'clock at night—we're grateful for practical options. Throw together this quick and easy soup when evening panic sets in.

3 tomatoes, coarsely chopped

6 celery stalks, coarsely chopped

Freshly squeezed lime or lemon juice (optional)

Dash hot pepper sauce

Put the tomatoes and celery in a blender. Process on low speed and gradually increase the speed until the vegetables are slightly chunky. Transfer the soup to a serving bowl and stir in the optional lime juice and hot pepper sauce. To serve warm, heat the soup in a small pot. To serve cold, chill it in the refrigerator.

out-of-the-red BEET SOUP

MAKES 3 SERVINGS   **$1.00** PER SERVING

Beets are easy to grow, making them a very economical choice, even if you buy them from someone else's garden.

> **2 cups shredded fresh beets**
>
> **1 cup unsweetened soymilk or rice milk**
>
> **2 tablespoons apple juice concentrate**
>
> **1½ teaspoons fresh dill, or ½ teaspoon dried dill weed, plus more for garnish**
>
> **1 teaspoon balsamic vinegar**

Put all the ingredients in a blender and process on high speed for 2 to 3 minutes, until completely smooth. Transfer to a medium saucepan and cook over medium heat until the soup is hot and steaming, about 10 minutes. Serve hot.

TIPS

- Choose beets that have healthy-looking greens attached, and you'll get two vegetables for the price of one. The nutritious beet greens can be steamed and served as a side dish.

- If you have a high-powered blender, such as a Vitamix, instead of heating the blended soup, heat the soymilk in a small saucepan before adding it to the blender. The friction from the blender will heat the soup to serving temperature.

- If you are using fresh dill, reserve a few sprigs to garnish each serving.

CALCIUM-RICH *kale soup*

$.75 PER SERVING   **MAKES 8 SERVINGS**

If you grow kale in your garden, even three-year-old children will be able to identify it and joyously pick it, eat it, and love it.

½ cup chopped leeks or green onions

½ red bell pepper, chopped

⅓ cup sliced almonds

4 cups water

6 to 8 tomatoes, chopped, or 1 can (14.5 ounces) **unsalted diced tomatoes, undrained**

2 tablespoons vegetable broth powder

1 tablespoon sweet paprika

2 bay leaves

2 cups chopped kale

1 cup cooked brown rice

1 cup cooked or canned garbanzo beans, drained and rinsed

Put the leeks, bell pepper, and almonds in a large soup pot over medium-high heat. Add 3 to 4 tablespoons of the water, 1 tablespoon at a time, and cook, stirring frequently, until the water evaporates and the onion is translucent. Stir in the remaining water, tomatoes, vegetable broth powder, paprika, and bay leaves and bring to a boil. Stir in the kale, rice, and beans. Decrease the heat to medium-low and simmer for 10 minutes, or until thoroughly heated. Remove the bay leaves. Serve hot.

cuban black bean SOUP

MAKES 4 SERVINGS   **$.50** PER SERVING

In this Caribbean classic, black beans are traditionally used to make a little meat go a long way when it's in short supply or too expensive. You'll never miss the meat in this version; the soup is quite tasty without it.

⅔ cup dried black beans, picked over, rinsed, and soaked (see page 19)

2 cups water

1 white onion, chopped, 2 tablespoons reserved for garnish

1 small green bell pepper, chopped

3 garlic cloves, minced

1 tablespoon vegetable broth powder

1 can (14.5 ounces) **unsalted diced tomatoes, or 1 can** (6 ounces) **unsalted tomato paste** (optional)

1 can (4 ounces) **diced green chiles, undrained**

1 teaspoon ground cumin

Drain the beans and put them in a large soup pot. Add the water and bring to a boil over medium-high heat. Decrease the heat to medium-low, cover, and cook for 1½ hours, or until the beans are tender. When the beans are cooked, stir in the onion, bell pepper, garlic, and vegetable broth powder. Increase the heat to high and cook, stirring frequently, for about 5 minutes. Stir in the optional tomatoes, chiles, and cumin. Decrease the heat to low and simmer, stirring occasionally, for about 15 minutes, or until the flavors are blended. Serve hot, garnished with the reserved onion.

TIP: This soup will keep for 1 week in the refrigerator, so double the recipe if you like.

MINESTRONE *with pasta shells*

I've modeled this soup after one served at my favorite restaurant. However, I left out the salt that keeps me thirsty for hours and the $3-per-cup price tag.

½ cup dried kidney beans, picked over, rinsed, and soaked
(see page 19)

½ cup dried great northern or cannellini beans, picked over, rinsed, and soaked (see page 19)

6 cups water

8 to 10 large tomatoes, finely chopped, or 1 can (28 ounces) **unsalted diced tomatoes, undrained**

1 onion, chopped

4 celery stalks, chopped

3 carrots, chopped

¼ head napa or green cabbage, chopped

½ cup cut green beans, fresh or frozen

2 tablespoons vegetable broth powder

2 garlic cloves, minced

4 ounces whole wheat pasta shells, elbow macaroni, or other small pasta

2 tablespoons chopped fresh parsley

Drain the beans and put them in a large soup pot. Add the water and bring to a boil over medium-high heat. Decrease the heat to medium-low, cover, and cook for 1 hour. Stir in the tomatoes, onion, celery, carrots, cabbage, green beans, vegetable broth powder, and garlic. Cover and cook, stirring occasionally, for about 30 minutes, until the beans and vegetables are tender. Stir in the pasta and cook until tender, about 10 minutes. Stir in the parsley. Serve hot.

VARIATION: Substitute up to 1 cup of chopped kale, spinach, or turnip greens for the cabbage. If you use fresh spinach, it will only take 1 to 2 minutes to cook. To avoid overcooking, stir in the spinach after the pasta is cooked.

delectable lentil SOUP

Lentils are the fastest-cooking legumes. They are tasty and meaty all on their own, but in this recipe, they are standouts.

7 cups water

½ pound yukon gold potatoes, cubed

1 cup green or brown lentils

1 onion, chopped

2 carrots, chopped

2 celery stalks, chopped

3 bay leaves

2 tablespoons vegetable broth powder

4 garlic cloves, minced

1 teaspoon dried basil

1 teaspoon dried oregano

½ teaspoon crushed dried rosemary

1 can (14.5 ounces) **unsalted crushed tomatoes** (preferably fire-roasted), **undrained**

Ground pepper

2 teaspoons red wine vinegar

Salt

Put the water, potatoes, lentils, onion, carrots, celery, bay leaves, vegetable broth powder, garlic, basil, oregano, and rosemary in a large soup pot. Bring to a boil over high heat, stirring occasionally. Decrease the heat to low, cover, and cook, stirring frequently, for 35 to 45 minutes, or until the lentils are tender. Add additional water if the soup is too thick. Stir in the tomatoes and pepper to taste. Cook, uncovered, for at least 15 minutes, stirring frequently to prevent the soup from sticking to the bottom of the pot and adding more water if the soup is too thick. Remove the bay leaves and stir in the vinegar and salt to taste. Serve hot.

TIP: This recipe can easily be made in a slow cooker—it will take 6 to 7 hours to cook on the low setting. Your kitchen will be filled with fragrant smells when you return hours later.

HEARTY *potato soup*

$.50 PER SERVING   **MAKES 6 SERVINGS**

This comforting soup has a creamy texture and packs a double dose of absorbable calcium, from the soymilk and the kale.

> 1 onion, chopped
>
> ½ cup water
>
> 1 garlic clove, minced
>
> 2 cups vegetable broth
>
> 1 russet potato, diced
>
> 1 sweet potato, peeled and diced
>
> 1 cup unsweetened soymilk or other nondairy milk
>
> 2 kale leaves, stemmed and chopped (about 2 cups)
>
> ¼ teaspoon curry powder
>
> ⅛ teaspoon ground turmeric

Put the onion, water, and garlic in a large soup pot over medium-high heat and bring to a boil. Decrease the heat to medium and cook, stirring occasionally, for about 5 minutes, or until the onion is soft. Stir in the broth, russet potato, and sweet potato. Cover and cook for about 15 minutes, or until the potatoes are tender when pierced with a fork. Pour half of the potato mixture into a blender, add the soymilk, and process until smooth. Set aside.

Add the kale, curry powder, and turmeric to the pot with the remaining potato mixture. Stir, cover, and cook over medium heat for about 5 minutes, or until the kale is tender. Stir the blended potato mixture into the soup pot and heat the soup thoroughly. Serve hot.

TIP: There is no need to peel the russet potatoes. You get extra fiber by leaving the skins on. Just scrub them well with a vegetable brush before using.

stone-broke SOUP

$.50 PER SERVING

This colorful vegetable soup features the same ingredients, minus the costly chicken, that are used in the popular children's story by a similar name.

8 cups water

2 russet potatoes, diced

3 tomatoes, chopped, or 1 can (14.5 ounces) unsalted diced tomatoes, undrained

2 onions, chopped

2 large carrots, cut into ½-inch thick slices

3 celery stalks, chopped

½ cup chopped fresh parsley

2 tablespoons vegetable broth powder

1 tablespoon chopped fresh basil, or 1 teaspoon dried

1 teaspoon dried marjoram

1 teaspoon dried thyme

1 bay leaf

½ cup brown rice or hulled barley

Salt

Ground pepper

Put the water, potatoes, tomatoes, onions, carrots, celery, parsley, vegetable broth powder, basil, marjoram, thyme, and bay leaf in a large soup pot over high heat and bring to a boil. Stir in the rice, cover, decrease the heat to low, and cook, stirring occasionally, for 1 hour. Remove the bay leaf and season with salt and pepper to taste. Serve hot.

TIPS

- If you're making this soup with children, you can add stones, just like in the story. Have your helpers find two round, smooth stones of a fairly good size (so they'll be easy to spot in the soup). Scrub the stones well and put them in the soup pot with the other ingredients. Just don't forget to remove them before serving!

- For more protein, add 2 cups of cooked beans.

- For a thicker soup, use more potatoes; for a thinner soup (or more servings), add more water.

- To prepare the soup in a slow cooker, combine all the ingredients and cook on low for 3 hours.

ITALIAN *carrot soup*

$.50 PER SERVING   **MAKES 12 SERVINGS**

This vibrantly colored, slightly sweet soup has less fat than typical creamy soups and provides an ample amount of beta-carotene.

1 tablespoon olive oil

2 pounds carrots, sliced

1 onion, chopped

6 cups water

2 large russet potatoes, diced

6 tablespoons vegetable broth powder

4 dates, pitted, or 1 tablespoon raisins

1 teaspoon italian seasoning

1 to 2 tablespoons chopped fresh parsley, for garnish

Salt

Ground pepper

Heat the oil in a large soup pot over medium heat. Add the carrots and onion and cook, stirring occasionally, for 5 to 10 minutes, until the onion is translucent. Stir in the water, potatoes, vegetable broth powder, dates, and italian seasoning. Cover and cook, stirring occasionally, until the vegetables are tender. Put half of the mixture in a blender and process until smooth. Pour the mixture into the pot and stir to blend. Serve hot, garnished with parsley. Pass salt and pepper at the table.

TIPS

- To decrease the amount of fat in this recipe, cook the carrots and onion in 3 tablespoons of water instead of the oil.
- Substitute 2 teaspoons of blackstrap molasses for the dates or raisins to sweeten this soup.

in the clover
salads

five-ingredient SALAD *for pennies*

25¢ 25¢ 25¢	**$.75** PER SERVING, DEPENDING ON INGREDIENTS USED	**MAKES 1 SERVING**

To make salad affordable, combine any five ingredients from the list below. There is no hard rule that says you have to eat leafy greens in a salad. For $.75 per serving, you get the basics. For another dime, you can add one-half cup of beans.

Salad greens (for example, arugula, baby spinach, or mixed greens), **rinsed, dried, and torn into bite-sized pieces**

Alfalfa sprouts

Bean sprouts

Black beans

Broccoli florets

Carrot, shredded

Cucumber, thinly sliced

Dried cherries

Dried cranberries

Edamame, shelled frozen, refrigerated, or fresh

Garbanzo beans

Kidney beans

Olives, pitted and sliced

Radishes, thinly sliced

Raisins

Red cabbage, shredded

Red onion, thinly sliced or diced

Summer squash, thinly sliced

Sundried tomatoes

Sunflower seeds

Tempeh (plain or flavored), cooked

Tofu (plain or flavored), crumbled

Tomato, sliced

Vegan cheese, shredded

Walnuts, chopped

Zucchini, thinly sliced

Pick 5 ingredients with different colors, flavors, and textures. For each serving, combine 1 cup of greens, if using, and 2 to 4 tablespoons each of the other ingredients in a large salad bowl. Add 2 tablespoons of a prepared salad dressing, or any of the salad dressings on pages 62 to 71, and toss to coat evenly.

TIPS

- So that the salad is easy to assemble at mealtimes, prepare fresh ingredients right after shopping. For example, wash and dry the greens, wash and cut the broccoli into florets, and shred the cabbage. Store the prepared ingredients in separate containers in the refrigerator so that they're ready to toss together or combine with pantry items.

- The salad can be assembled and stored in the refrigerator, without dressing, for 2 days. Tomatoes should be kept separately and added shortly before serving.

checkbook-saving BEAN SALAD

MAKES 8 SERVINGS   **$.50** PER SERVING

Full of fiber and flavor, this is a versatile salad that you can serve as a side dish, light lunch, or snack.

> **2 cucumbers, cubed**
>
> **2 tomatoes, cubed**
>
> **1¾ cups cooked or canned garbanzo beans, drained and rinsed**
>
> **½ onion, minced**
>
> **2½ tablespoons chopped fresh mint**
>
> **2 tablespoons freshly squeezed lemon juice or fruit-infused vinegar**
>
> **1 tablespoon extra-virgin olive oil** (optional)
>
> **2 garlic cloves, minced**
>
> **8 leaves red leaf lettuce, torn**

Put the cucumbers, tomatoes, beans, onion, mint, lemon juice, optional oil, and garlic in a large salad bowl and toss to combine. Chill for at least 15 minutes. Place the lettuce leaves on a serving platter or individual salad plates. Spoon the salad onto the leaves.

TIPS

- First try this recipe without the oil, then add it only if you must.
- Tasty fruit-infused vinegars are available at grocery stores and online.

GARBANZO *bean salad*

This is a light and refreshing salad that gets a touch of sweetness from raisins and maple syrup.

2 tablespoons freshly squeezed lime or lemon juice

2 tablespoons extra-virgin olive oil (optional)

2 teaspoons curry powder

2 teaspoons maple syrup

2 teaspoons cider vinegar

½ teaspoon salt

3½ cups cooked or canned garbanzo beans, drained and rinsed

1 red bell pepper, chopped

⅔ cup finely chopped red onion

½ cup chopped fresh cilantro or parsley

½ cup raisins

2 teaspoons cumin seeds, toasted (see tips)

8 cups mixed salad greens

1 whole wheat pita bread, sliced into 8 wedges and toasted

Put the lime juice, optional oil, curry powder, maple syrup, vinegar, and salt in a large salad bowl and whisk to blend. Add the beans, bell pepper, onion, cilantro, raisins, and cumin seeds and toss to combine. Place the salad greens on a serving platter or individual salad plates. Spoon the salad onto the greens. Serve the toasted pita wedges with the salad.

TIPS

- To toast the cumin seeds, put the seeds in a small skillet or saucepan over medium heat. Cook and stir for 3 to 5 minutes, or until the seeds turn a shade darker, start to crackle, and are aromatic.
- The easiest way to toast the pita wedges is in a toaster oven.

community garden SALAD

This salad features hardy autumn vegetables that are easy to grow in a home or community garden. They hold up well, even in cold temperatures.

> ½ **head romaine lettuce, torn into bite-sized pieces**
> ½ **head cauliflower, shredded or chopped**
> 1 **beet, shredded**
> 1 **carrot, shredded**
> 1 **radish, shredded**
> **Salad dressing** (see tips)

Put all the ingredients in a large salad bowl. Add salad dressing to taste and toss to coat.

TIPS

- It takes only about 30 seconds to shred the beet, carrot, and radish in a food processor with a shredding disk. It takes a few more seconds using a mandoline or manual shredder. A sharp knife will also work just fine.

- Use your favorite bottled salad dressing or one of the salad dressing recipes on pages 62 to 71.

EASY *bean salad*

$.75 PER SERVING   **MAKES 10 SERVINGS**

Having a salad without lettuce or greens can be a refreshing change. That said, it is a good idea to eat leafy greens every day if you can. A good compromise is to serve this salad over a bed of romaine leaves or a spring lettuce mix.

3 cups cooked or canned black-eyed peas, drained and rinsed

3 cups cooked or canned kidney beans, drained and rinsed

3 cups cooked or canned pinto beans, drained and rinsed

1 package (10 ounces) **frozen fordhook lima beans, thawed**

1 cup frozen corn, thawed, or ½ **can** (8 ounces) **corn, rinsed and drained**

1 small red bell pepper, diced

½ **red onion, diced**

½ **cup low-fat italian salad dressing**

Salt

Ground pepper

Put the black-eyed peas, kidney beans, pinto beans, lima beans, corn, bell pepper, and onion in a large salad bowl and mix well. Add the dressing and stir to coat the vegetables and beans thoroughly. Season with salt and pepper to taste.

TIP: During the summer when it is in season, fresh corn on the cob is much cheaper than canned or frozen. To replace the frozen corn in Easy Bean Salad, steam 1 or 2 ears for 10 to 15 minutes, or until just tender, and remove the kernels. Fresh corn adds a natural, crunchy sweetness and tastes oh-so-much better.

SEAWEED *salad*

MAKES 1 SERVING   **$3.00** PER SERVING

This salad is reminiscent of the small bowls of crunchy marinated sea vegetables served in Japanese restaurants.

- ⅜ **ounce dried wakame or hijiki**
- 3 **tablespoons unseasoned rice vinegar**
- 3 **tablespoons low-sodium soy sauce**
- 2 **tablespoons sesame oil**
- 1 **teaspoon finely grated fresh ginger**
- 1 **teaspoon sugar or other sweetener**
- ¼ **cucumber, thinly sliced** (optional)
- 1 **tablespoon sesame seeds, toasted**
- 2 **green onions, thinly sliced**

Put the dried wakame in a medium bowl. Cover with warm water and let soak for 5 to 8 minutes. Hold the soaking wakame with one hand, and with the other hand turn the bowl upside down to drain. Cover the wakame with fresh warm water and drain. Fill another medium bowl with very cold water. Quickly immerse the wakame in the cold water and drain well. Put the wakame in a small bowl. Set aside.

To make the dressing, combine the vinegar, soy sauce, oil, ginger, and sugar in a small bowl and whisk until the sugar is dissolved. Pour the dressing over the wakame, add the optional cucumber, and mix well. Sprinkle with the sesame seeds and green onions. Serve immediately or refrigerate until needed.

strawberry and citrus SALAD

$2.50 PER SERVING

MAKES 4 SERVINGS

Bright and tangy, this salad features a wonderful contrast in textures, with tender greens, juicy fruit, and crunchy nuts.

2 cups fresh strawberries

1 bag (10 ounces) **spinach, torn into bite-sized pieces**

1 head bibb lettuce, or ½ head boston lettuce, torn into bite-sized pieces

2 tangerines or clementines, separated into sections, or 1 can (4 ounces) **mandarin oranges, drained**

1 sweet onion, thinly sliced

Salad dressing (see tips)

¼ cup chopped walnuts, for garnish

Save 6 to 8 whole strawberries for the garnish and cut the remaining berries in half. Combine the spinach, lettuce, halved strawberries, tangerines, and onions in a large salad bowl. Add salad dressing to taste and toss to coat. Transfer individual portions to 4 small plates. Garnish with the whole strawberries and walnuts.

TIPS

- If you can't find bibb or boston lettuce, romaine will work as well.
- Use your favorite bottled salad dressing or one of the salad dressing recipes on pages 62 to 71.
- This salad can be stored in the refrigerator, without the dressing, for 2 to 3 days, if tightly covered.

tropical SALAD

MAKES 4 SERVINGS   **$1.25** PER SERVING

The sweet juices of the tomatoes and mangoes, along with the rich flavors of the coconut and cilantro, make it unnecessary to add dressing to this salad.

8 leaves romaine lettuce

2 mangoes, peeled, seeded, and chopped (3 to 4 cups)

2 tomatoes, diced

½ small red onion, thinly sliced

2 tablespoons chopped fresh cilantro

1 tablespoon unsweetened flaked coconut

Tear each lettuce leaf in half horizontally. Place the dark-green tops of the leaves on a serving platter or individual salad plates. Tear the remaining bottoms of the leaves into bite-sized pieces and put them in a large bowl. Add the mangoes, tomatoes, onion, cilantro, and coconut and gently toss with two forks until well combined. Spoon the mango mixture onto the lettuce leaves.

TIP: Substitute 3 to 4 cups of thawed frozen mango chunks for the fresh mangoes.

tabouli

Abundant amounts of fresh parsley and mint make this salad particularly refreshing.

2 cups medium-grind bulgur

2 cups very hot water

½ cup freshly squeezed lemon juice

¼ cup extra-virgin olive oil (optional)

1 garlic clove, minced (optional)

Salt

Ground pepper

2 small tomatoes, chopped

2 cups chopped fresh parsley

8 green onions, sliced

½ cup chopped fresh mint

1 cucumber, quartered lengthwise and cut into ¼-inch-thick slices

Put the bulgur and hot water in a large bowl, cover, and let sit for about 30 minutes, or until all the water is absorbed. While the bulgur is soaking, make a dressing by combining the lemon juice, optional oil, optional garlic, and salt and pepper to taste in a small bowl. Whisk until well blended. Set aside.

Fluff the bulgur with a fork. Stir in the tomatoes, parsley, green onions, mint, and cucumber. Pour on the dressing and toss to coat. Serve chilled or at room temperature.

TIP: Tabouli is often considered a side dish, but you can turn it into a main course by adding 2 cups of garbanzo beans, which will give you protein and good-for-you complex carbohydrates.

working lunch SALAD AND DRESSING

MAKES 4 SERVINGS **$.75** PER SERVING

When you're stuck in the office all day, you may not be able to buy a really fresh salad for lunch. Take a little time in the morning or even the night before to prepare a salad like this one and brown-bag an affordable, healthful meal.

SALAD

1 medium head lettuce, such as red leaf, romaine, or a combination, torn into bite-sized pieces

2 cups cooked or canned garbanzo beans or other beans, drained and rinsed

2 tomatoes, diced

2 carrots, shredded

DRESSING

½ onion, finely minced

3 tablespoons freshly squeezed lemon juice

2 garlic cloves, minced

½ teaspoon chopped fresh mint, cilantro, or basil

Salt

Ground pepper

To make the salad, put the lettuce, beans, tomatoes, and carrots in a large salad bowl.

To make the dressing, put the onion, lemon juice, garlic, mint, and salt and pepper to taste in a cruet or small jar and seal tightly. Shake well before using. Dress the salad just before eating.

TIPS

- Add any extra vegetables you have in the refrigerator, such as broccoli florets, sliced cucumbers, a few olives, or sliced zucchini.
- This salad can be assembled and stored in the refrigerator, without dressing, for 2 days. Tomatoes should be kept separately and added shortly before serving.
- Serve this salad with whole-grain bread or rolled up like a wrap in a sprouted whole-grain tortilla.

strike it rich
salad dressings

SALAD DRESSINGS

BASIC *mustard dressing*

$.25 PER SERVING   **MAKES ABOUT ¼ CUP (2 SERVINGS)**

Even if you're not a mustard fan, try this dressing. You may be surprised by how well the mustard and vinegar flavors go together.

2 tablespoons extra-virgin olive oil

2 tablespoons sesame seeds, toasted (optional; see tips)

1 tablespoon freshly squeezed lemon juice

1 tablespoon cider vinegar

1 teaspoon dijon mustard

1 garlic clove, minced (optional)

Salt

Ground pepper

Put the oil, optional sesame seeds, lemon juice, vinegar, mustard, optional garlic, and salt and pepper to taste in a small bowl and whisk to combine. Pour into a cruet or small jar and seal tightly. Shake well before using. Stored in the refrigerator, Basic Mustard Dressing will keep for about 2 weeks.

TIPS

- To decrease the fat in this recipe, replace half the oil with water, or replace all the oil with 1 tablespoon of water and a second tablespoon of vinegar.
- To toast the sesame seeds, put the seeds in a small skillet or saucepan over medium heat. Cook and stir for 3 to 5 minutes, or until the seeds turn a shade darker, start to crackle, and are aromatic.

basic oil-and-vinegar DRESSING

MAKES ABOUT ½ CUP (4 SERVINGS)　　　　**$.25** PER SERVING　

Nothing could be simpler than this dressing, which goes well with a wide variety of greens.

> **6 tablespoons freshly squeezed lemon juice or vinegar of choice**
>
> **3 tablespoons extra-virgin olive oil**
>
> **2 tablespoons chopped fresh parsley**
>
> **¼ teaspoon onion powder**

Put all the ingredients in a cruet or small jar and seal tightly. Shake well before using. Stored in the refrigerator, Basic Oil-and-Vinegar Dressing will keep for about 1 week.

TIP: To decrease the fat in this recipe, increase the lemon and decrease the oil to taste.

caesar DRESSING

Most recipes for caesar dressing are not vegetarian, let alone vegan, because they contain anchovies. This easy-to-make dressing packs in the flavor without the fish.

¼ cup pine nuts or sliced almonds (see tips)

¼ cup water

2 tablespoons freshly squeezed lemon juice

2 tablespoons dijon mustard

2 tablespoons nutritional yeast flakes

1 tablespoon extra-virgin olive oil or vegan sour cream

1½ teaspoons low-sodium soy sauce or Bragg Liquid Aminos

2 garlic cloves, minced

1 teaspoon onion powder

Salt

Ground pepper

Put all the ingredients in a blender or food processor. Pulse the blender on and off for 1 to 2 minutes, just until the dressing is creamy. Pour into a cruet or small jar and seal tightly. Shake well before using. Stored in the refrigerator, Caesar Dressing will keep for about 2 weeks.

TIPS

- This dressing goes well on a traditional caesar salad made of romaine lettuce and whole wheat croutons with slices of tomato or avocado.

- If time permits, soak the pine nuts in a small bowl of water for at least 1 hour before making this dressing. Alternatively, put the pine nuts in a small skillet and add enough water just to cover. Lightly steam over medium heat for 1 minute and drain.

- If made with the vegan sour cream instead of the olive oil, this dressing will keep in the refrigerator for 4 to 5 days.

fragrant VINAIGRETTE

MAKES ABOUT 1 CUP (8 SERVINGS)   **$.25** PER SERVING

This herb-filled vinaigrette tastes just right with tender baby lettuces.

- **½ cup freshly squeezed lemon juice**
- **½ cup raspberry vinegar**
- **1 green onion, finely chopped**
- **1 tablespoon chopped fresh parsley**
- **2 teaspoons grainy dijon mustard**
- **1 teaspoon finely chopped fresh basil**
- **Salt**
- **Ground pepper**

Put the lemon juice, vinegar, green onion, parsley, mustard, and basil in a blender or food processor and process until well combined. Season with salt and pepper to taste. Pour into a cruet or small jar and seal tightly. Shake well before using. Stored in the refrigerator, Fragrant Vinaigrette will keep for 3 to 4 days.

TIP: Try substituting another flavored vinegar for the raspberry vinegar. Some delicious choices include cider vinegar, blood orange- or pear-infused vinegars, or riesling vinegar. In fact, many vinegars are so flavorful, they can dress a salad on their own—simply pour the vinegar into a clean spray bottle and spritz the salad.

LEMONY *dressing*

$.25 PER SERVING   **MAKES ABOUT 1 CUP** (8 SERVINGS)

Dates take the place of other sweeteners in this sweet-and-sour dressing.

⅓ **cup freshly squeezed lemon juice**

⅓ **cup extra-virgin olive oil**

⅓ **cup water**

1 **tablespoon chopped dates**

1 **teaspoon minced fresh tarragon**

⅛ **teaspoon ground black pepper**

Put all the ingredients in a blender or food processor and process until smooth. Pour into a cruet or small jar and seal tightly. Shake well before using. Stored in the refrigerator, Lemony Dressing will keep for about 1 week.

TIPS

- If you don't have dates, use 1 tablespoon of maple syrup or agave nectar instead.
- Decrease the amount of oil in this recipe if you can do without it.

garlic-lime DRESSING

MAKES ABOUT ⅔ CUP (5 SERVINGS) **LESS THAN $.25** PER SERVING

In this dressing, fresh lime balances the pungent taste of the garlic and shallots.

> ⅓ **cup freshly squeezed lime juice**
>
> ¼ **cup extra-virgin olive oil**
>
> **1 shallot, chopped**
>
> **1 garlic clove, chopped**
>
> **Salt**
>
> **Ground pepper**

Put all the ingredients in a blender or food processor and process until smooth. Pour into a cruet or small jar and seal tightly. Shake well before using. Stored in the refrigerator, Garlic-Lime Dressing will keep for about 1 week.

TIPS

- Often used in French, Indonesian, and Thai cooking, shallots have thin brown skins and an elongated shape. They look like large, brown-skinned garlic cloves. Their flavor is frequently described as a cross between sweet onions and garlic. If you can't find shallots, use 2 additional garlic cloves instead.

- To decrease the fat in this dressing, replace the oil with 2 additional tablespoons of lime juice and 2 tablespoons of water.

FAT-FREE *russian dressing*

If you can't find a tasty no-fat russian dressing at the grocery store, this recipe may be the answer to your prayers.

1 large tomato, chopped

½ cup freshly squeezed lemon juice

1 small green onion, chopped, or 1 teaspoon onion powder

1 tablespoon agave nectar or maple syrup

1 teaspoon grated horseradish

1 teaspoon sweet paprika

1 garlic clove

Put all the ingredients in a blender or food processor and process until smooth. Pour into a cruet or small jar and seal tightly. Shake well before using. Stored in the refrigerator, Fat-Free Russian Dressing will keep for 2 to 3 days.

TIP: If you don't have a fresh tomato, use 2 whole canned tomatoes or 1 cup of thick tomato juice instead.

EASY *miso dressing*

MAKES ABOUT ½ CUP (4 SERVINGS) **$.25** PER SERVING

This classic dressing can make a simple bed of lettuce leaves come alive. Add more water for a thinner consistency and to make the dressing stretch further.

> **2 tablespoons miso, any variety**
>
> **2 tablespoons rice vinegar**
>
> **2 tablespoons low-sodium soy sauce**
>
> **1 tablespoon sesame oil**
>
> **½ teaspoon grated fresh ginger, or 1 teaspoon ground ginger**

Put all the ingredients in a blender or food processor and process until smooth. For a thinner dressing, add water, 1 teaspoon at a time, until the desired consistency is achieved. Pour into a cruet or small jar and seal tightly. Shake well before using. Stored in the refrigerator, Easy Miso Dressing will keep for about 2 weeks.

TIP: For a sweeter dressing, add a few raisins before processing.

SUPERSWEET *dressing*

LESS THAN **$.25** PER SERVING 25¢ **MAKES ABOUT 1 CUP (8 SERVINGS)**

If you have a sweet tooth, this dressing is guaranteed to wake up your taste buds and enhance your appreciation of salad greens and vegetables.

> **1 can** (8 ounces) **pineapple chunks, packed in juice, undrained**
> **2 celery stalks**

Put all the ingredients in a blender or food processor and process until smooth. Pour into a cruet or small jar and seal tightly. Shake well before using. Stored in the refrigerator, Supersweet Dressing will keep for 4 days.

creamy tahini DRESSING

MAKES ABOUT 1½ CUPS (12 SERVINGS)　　　LESS THAN **$.25** PER SERVING

This tahini dressing is different than most because it contains beans and balsamic vinegar. The beans give the dressing a creamier, thicker texture and make the recipe stretch further.

> **1¾ cups cooked or canned garbanzo beans, drained and rinsed**
>
> **1 tablespoon tahini**
>
> **2 teaspoons balsamic vinegar**
>
> **1 teaspoon low-sodium soy sauce**
>
> **1 garlic clove**

Put all the ingredients in a blender or food processor and process until smooth. For a thinner dressing, add water, 1 tablespoon at a time, until the desired consistency is achieved. Transfer to a cruet, small jar, or storage container and seal tightly. Shake or stir well before using. Stored in the refrigerator, Creamy Tahini Dressing will keep for about 5 days.

TIP: Canned beans have plenty of salt. If you use cooked dried beans, you may want to add salt to taste.

save the day
entrées

ENTRÉES

CHUNKY *chili*

$1.00 PER SERVING   **MAKES 8 SERVINGS**

This recipe features bulgur, a form of cracked wheat. Add vegan burger crumbles for a more traditional flavor and texture.

1 tablespoon olive oil or water

3 onions, chopped

3 garlic cloves, minced

1 package (12 ounces) **vegan burger crumbles** (optional)

1 tablespoon chili powder

1 tablespoon ground cumin

¼ teaspoon cayenne

2 green bell peppers, chopped

1 can (28 ounces) **unsalted diced tomatoes, undrained**

1 cup water

2 cups frozen corn

1¾ cups cooked or canned black beans, drained and rinsed

1¾ cups cooked or canned red kidney beans, drained and rinsed

½ cup medium-grind bulgur

Salt

Ground pepper

1 avocado, sliced, for garnish

Chopped fresh cilantro, for garnish

Heat the oil in a large soup pot over medium heat. Add the onions, garlic, optional vegan burger crumbles, chili powder, cumin, and cayenne and cook, stirring occasionally, for 5 minutes, or until the vegetables are soft and translucent. Stir in the bell peppers and cook for 1 minute. Stir in the tomatoes with their liquid and the water. Increase the heat to high and bring to a boil. Stir in the corn, black beans, kidney beans, and bulgur. Decrease the heat to low and cook, uncovered, for 15 minutes, stirring occasionally. Season with salt and pepper to taste.

Serve hot, garnished with the avocado slices and cilantro.

VARIATION: Substitute 12 ounces of sliced mushrooms for the optional vegan burger crumbles.

pot-of-gold rainbow STEW

MAKES 8 SERVINGS   **$1.50** PER SERVING

You'll save a pot of gold when you opt for this multihued bean and vegetable stew instead of a traditional meat-laden stew.

1 cup dried pinto beans, picked over, rinsed, and soaked (see page XX)

3¼ cups water

2 onions, chopped

1 eggplant, quartered lengthwise and cut into ½-inch-thick slices

1 green bell pepper, diced

5 garlic cloves, minced

3 small zucchini, quartered lengthwise and cut into ½-inch-thick slices

1 red bell pepper, coarsely chopped

1 cup chopped fresh basil

Salt

Ground pepper

Drain the soaked beans and put them in a large saucepan. Add 3 cups of the water and bring to a boil over medium-high heat. Decrease the heat to medium-low, cover, and cook for 1 to 1½ hours, or until tender. Set aside; do not drain.

While the beans cook, put 1 tablespoon of the remaining water and the onions in a large soup pot and cook over medium-high heat, stirring frequently, for about 5 minutes, or until the onions are translucent. Stir in the eggplant, green bell pepper, garlic, and the remaining water, 1 tablespoon at a time, as it evaporates. Cover and cook, stirring occasionally, for 5 to 10 minutes, or until the eggplant begins to soften. Stir in the zucchini, red bell pepper, and basil. Cover and cook, stirring occasionally, for about 3 minutes, or until the vegetables are tender. Stir in the cooked beans and bean liquid. Season with salt and pepper to taste.

TIP: Substitute 1 can (15 ounces) of pinto beans instead of cooking the beans yourself. Rinse and drain the beans. Stir the beans and an additional ¼ cup of water into the vegetable mixture.

RICE *and* BEANS, *rice* AND *beans*

$.25 PER SERVING   **MAKES 10 SERVINGS**

If you remember nothing else, please take away the mantra from the recipe title above: "rice and beans, rice and beans." You get more calories, fiber, iron, vitamins, and bang for your buck from this food combination than from any other I can think of.

4 cups plus 5 tablespoons water

2 cups long-grain brown rice

1 small yellow onion, chopped

½ red or green bell pepper, chopped

6 tablespoons chopped fresh cilantro

2 garlic cloves, minced

1 tablespoon vegan worcestershire sauce (optional)

2 cups dried black beans, cooked (see page 19), **or 2 cans** (15 ounces each) **black beans, drained, liquid reserved**

Salt

Ground pepper

Put 4 cups of the water in a large pot and bring to a boil. Stir in the rice and return to a boil. Decrease the heat to low, cover, and cook for about 45 minutes, or until the rice is almost tender and the water is just absorbed. Remove from the heat and let sit for 5 minutes. Uncover and fluff with a fork. Set aside.

Put 3 tablespoons of the remaining water, the onion, bell pepper, 2 tablespoons of the cilantro, and the garlic in a large skillet and cook, stirring frequently, over medium-high heat for 8 to 10 minutes, or until the onion and garlic are translucent. Add the remaining water, 1 tablespoon at a time, as it evaporates.

Combine the vegetable mixture with the rice in the rice pot and mix well. Gently stir in the optional vegan worcestershire sauce, beans, and about ½ cup of bean liquid. Cook, stirring occasionally, for 2 to 3 minutes. Stir in the remaining 4 tablespoons of cilantro. Season with salt and pepper to taste.

TIP: This recipe calls for an equal amount of rice and beans. However, to stretch your food dollars, increase the ratio of rice to beans to 2:1 or even 4:1. The dish will still have plenty of protein.

creamy noodle **CASSEROLE**

The vegan sour cream in this recipe gives it a rich, thick, and creamy sauce.

4 ounces flat whole wheat noodles

1 tablespoon vegetable oil

1 package (12 ounces) **vegan burger crumbles**

1 onion, chopped

1 container (12 ounces) **vegan sour cream**

1½ cups water

3 carrots, thinly sliced

2 tomatoes, chopped

2 tablespoons vegetable broth powder

1 tablespoon chopped fresh marjoram, or 1 teaspoon dried

1 tablespoon chopped fresh sage, or 1 teaspoon dried

¼ teaspoon ground black pepper

½ cup whole-grain oat crackers

⅓ cup chopped pecans or walnuts

2 tablespoons nonhydrogenated vegan margarine, melted

Heat the oven to 375 degrees F.

Cook the noodles according to the package directions, drain in a colander, and set aside.

While the noodles are cooking, heat the oil in a 12-inch skillet over medium heat. Add the vegan burger crumbles and onion and cook, stirring frequently, for 10 minutes. Stir in the vegan sour cream, water, carrots, tomatoes, vegetable broth powder, marjoram, sage, and pepper. Cook, stirring occasionally, for 5 minutes, or until the carrots are just tender.

Transfer the noodles to a 6-cup nonstick casserole (or a glass casserole lightly coated with nonstick cooking spray). Stir in the vegan burger crumble mixture until well combined. Cover the casserole with a lid or aluminum foil and bake for 30 minutes.

While the casserole bakes, crumble the crackers into small crumbs in a small bowl. Add the pecans and vegan margarine and mix well. Remove the casserole from the oven, remove the foil, and sprinkle the crumb mixture evenly over the top. Bake, uncovered, for 5 to 10 minutes, or until the topping looks crunchy and brown.

TIP: Don't have vegan sour cream on hand? No problem. You can make this casserole without it, but the tomato flavor will be more prominent.

SAVE-CASH *quinoa loaf*

$.75 PER SERVING

MAKES 8 SERVINGS

Fiber, protein, and vegetables are all rolled into one in this flavor-packed loaf. Add a leafy salad for an affordable, satisfying dinner.

½ cup plus 3 tablespoons water

8 ounces white button mushrooms, sliced

1¾ cups cooked or canned garbanzo beans, drained and rinsed

¾ cup rolled oats

2 cups cooked quinoa

1 cup frozen green peas

½ cup chopped fresh parsley, or 1 tablespoon minced fresh thyme, or both

10 sundried tomatoes, soaked in water for 1 hour, drained, and chopped

½ cup chopped red onion (about ½ onion)

Salt

Ground pepper

Preheat the oven to 350 degrees F. Lightly coat an 8-inch loaf pan with nonstick cooking spray or olive oil.

Put 1 tablespoon of the water and the mushrooms in a large skillet and cook, stirring occasionally, over medium-high heat for 6 to 8 minutes. Add 2 more tablespoons of the water, 1 tablespoon at a time, as it evaporates. Transfer the mushrooms to a large bowl and set aside.

Put the beans, oats, and remaining ½ cup water in a food processor and pulse until almost smooth. Combine the bean mixture, quinoa, peas, parsley, tomatoes, onion, and salt and pepper to taste with the mushrooms in the large bowl and stir well. Transfer the mixture to the prepared loaf pan and gently press down. Bake for 1 to 1¼ hours, or until firm and golden brown. Remove from the oven and cool for 10 minutes before slicing and serving.

TIP: Leftover slices are delectable in sandwiches or stuffed into whole wheat pita bread.

beans-and-greens STIR-FRY

This colorful and fiber-rich stir-fry is easy to prepare. If you happen to have leftover rice, you can get the stir-fry on the table in a flash.

⅔ cup plus ¼ cup water

⅓ cup brown rice

1¾ cups cooked or canned black beans, drained and rinsed

2 teaspoons dried onion flakes, plus more for garnish

1 teaspoon ground cumin

Pinch crushed red pepper flakes (optional)

1 teaspoon olive oil

1 garlic clove, minced

½ cup chopped broccoli

½ cup chopped collard greens

1 teaspoon low-sodium soy sauce

1 teaspoon fresh or dried parsley, plus more for garnish

Put ⅔ cup of the water in a medium saucepan and bring to a boil over high heat. Add the rice and return to a boil. Decrease the heat to low, cover, and cook for 45 minutes, or until the rice is tender and the water is absorbed. Set aside. Fluff with a fork before serving.

While the rice cooks, combine the beans, onion flakes, cumin, and optional red pepper flakes in a small saucepan over low heat. Cook, stirring frequently, until warmed through.

Heat the oil in a wok or large skillet over medium heat. Add the garlic and cook and stir for 1 minute. Stir in the broccoli and the remaining ¼ cup of water. Cover and cook for 2 to 3 minutes, or until the broccoli is bright green. Add the collard greens and cook, stirring frequently, for 3 to 5 minutes, or until the greens are wilted and tender. Stir in the soy sauce and parsley and remove from the heat. To serve, spoon portions of the rice onto two plates. Top the rice with the beans and greens. Sprinkle with additional onion flakes and parsley.

TIPS

- To save time, prepare the vegetables and other ingredients while the rice cooks or, for an even faster dinner, cook the rice in advance, refrigerate until needed, and reheat.

- This stir-fry works equally well when served over other whole grains.

royal STIR-FRY

There can be many variations to this theme, but here is a basic, nutritious stir-fry.

  2½ cups water

  1 cup brown rice

  2 tablespoons vegetable broth powder

  1¾ cups cooked or canned garbanzo beans, drained and rinsed

  ½ cup finely sliced broccoli

  ½ cup shredded cabbage

  ½ cup thinly sliced green beans

  ½ cup thinly sliced white button mushrooms

  1 carrot, sliced into matchsticks

  ½ onion, sliced into small wedges

  2 tablespoons low-sodium soy sauce

  Sesame seeds (optional)

Put 2 cups of the water in a medium saucepan and bring to a boil over high heat. Stir in the rice and return to a boil. Decrease the heat to low, cover, and cook for 45 minutes, or until the rice is tender and the water is absorbed. Fluff with a fork before serving.

Put ¼ cup of the water and the vegetable broth powder in a wok or large skillet, mix well, and bring to a boil over high heat. Decrease the heat to medium and stir in the garbanzo beans, broccoli, cabbage, green beans, mushrooms, carrot, and onion. Cover and cook, stirring occasionally to prevent sticking, for about 10 minutes, or until the vegetables are tender but still slightly crisp. If necessary, add the remaining water, 1 tablespoon at a time, to prevent sticking. Add the soy sauce and stir to combine.

Serve over the rice. Sprinkle with sesame seeds, if desired.

TIPS

- To save time, prepare the vegetables while the rice cooks. Slicing and shredding can be done very quickly if you use a food processor or mandoline.

- A good vegetable broth powder should include a variety of fragrant spices, but you can always add your own favorites, such as curry powder, garlic powder, or ground turmeric. Use just a pinch of each additional spice at a time until the desired flavor is achieved.

taste-of-thai SAUTÉ

MAKES 6 SERVINGS   **$1.50** PER SERVING

This colorful, creamy sauté has the rich flavors of your favorite restaurant takeout, but without the high price tag.

1 tablespoon vegetable oil	1 red bell pepper, finely chopped
1 onion, chopped	1 cup carrot slices
1 tablespoon minced fresh ginger	1 cup cut green beans
3 garlic cloves, minced	1 can (15 ounces) **light coconut milk**
¼ teaspoon crushed red pepper flakes	½ cup chopped fresh thai basil or sweet basil
1 teaspoon ground coriander	2 tablespoons low-sodium soy sauce
1 teaspoon ground cumin	1 tablespoon freshly squeezed lime juice
1 teaspoon ground turmeric	1 teaspoon agave nectar or maple syrup
1 eggplant, cut into bite-sized pieces	3 cups cooked brown rice or millet
2 cups cauliflower florets	

Heat the oil in a wok or large skillet over medium-high heat. Add the onion and ginger and cook and stir for 1 minute. Add the garlic and red pepper flakes and cook and stir for about 30 seconds, or until fragrant. Add the coriander, cumin, and turmeric and cook and stir for 30 seconds. Add the eggplant, cauliflower, bell pepper, carrot, and green beans and stir well to coat the vegetables with the seasonings. Stir in the coconut milk and bring to a boil. Decrease the heat to low and cook, uncovered, for 3 minutes, adding water if needed to keep the ingredients from sticking to the skillet. Cook, stirring occasionally, for 5 minutes, or until the vegetables are tender but not over-cooked. Add the basil, soy sauce, lime juice, and agave nectar and cook and stir for 1 minute.

Serve over the rice.

TIPS

- Shake the can of coconut milk before opening. To get the best flavor, open the coconut milk just before using.
- For a slightly different taste, add ½ teaspoon of curry powder to the vegetables while they are cooking.

tempeh-broccoli SAUTÉ

$1.25 PER SERVING

MAKES 4 SERVINGS

Tempeh, a very nutritious form of soy, is a wonderful source of fiber and protein. It has an earthy flavor that pairs well with strong seasonings, such as the garlic, ginger, and soy sauce in this recipe.

1 package (8 ounces) **tempeh, cut into** ½-**inch cubes**

1 cup water

1 cup chopped broccoli, or 1 package (8 ounces) **frozen broccoli florets**

1 small onion, minced

½ **red bell pepper, chopped**

3 garlic cloves, minced

1 teaspoon minced fresh ginger, or ½ **teaspoon ground ginger**

1 tablespoon low-sodium soy sauce

Put the tempeh and water in a large skillet and cook over medium heat for 10 minutes. Drain the tempeh in a colander, discarding the cooking water. Lightly coat the skillet with nonstick cooking spray. Put the tempeh, broccoli, onion, bell pepper, garlic, and ginger in the skillet and cook over medium-high heat for about 15 minutes, or until the tempeh is lightly browned. Stir in the soy sauce.

TIP: Tempeh-Broccoli Sauté can be served as a side dish or over brown rice as a main course.

SESAME *bok choy*

This recipe includes protein-rich quinoa and can be used either as an entrée or a side dish. Stored in the refrigerator, leftovers will keep for two to three days.

1 teaspoon toasted sesame oil

4 carrots, cut diagonally into ¼-inch slices

½ cup chopped green onions

6 garlic cloves, minced

6 cups chopped bok choy (2 to 3 large heads, or 4 to 6 "baby" heads)

½ cup water

1½ teaspoons vegetable broth powder

2 teaspoons low-sodium soy sauce

1 tablespoon minced fresh ginger

1 teaspoon agave nectar or maple syrup (optional)

3 cups cooked quinoa

3 tablespoons unsalted roasted sesame seeds

Heat the oil in a large nonstick skillet over medium heat. Add the carrots, green onions, and garlic and cook and stir for 3 minutes. Add the bok choy and cook and stir for 2 minutes. Stir in the water, vegetable broth powder, soy sauce, ginger, and optional agave nectar. Decrease the heat to low, cover, and cook for 5 minutes.

To serve, spoon over the cooked quinoa. Sprinkle with the sesame seeds.

TIP: Substitute cooked brown rice for the quinoa.

bean SANGWICHES

$1.00 PER SERVING   **MAKES 4 SERVINGS**

These tasty sandwiches are a convenient and wholesome alternative to fast food fare.

> 3½ cups cooked or canned garbanzo beans, drained and rinsed
>
> 1 large celery stalk, chopped
>
> 1 green onion, finely chopped
>
> 2 tablespoons vegan mayonnaise
>
> 1 tablespoon sweet pickle relish
>
> 8 slices whole wheat bread
>
> 4 lettuce leaves
>
> 4 tomato slices

Put the beans in a large bowl and mash them with a fork or potato masher, leaving some chunks. Stir in the celery, green onion, vegan mayonnaise, and relish and mix well. Spread one-quarter of the mixture evenly on 4 slices of the bread and top with the lettuce leaves, tomato slices, and remaining pieces of bread.

BILLFOLD-SAVER *black bean burgers*

MAKES 8 BURGERS (4 SERVINGS)   **$.50** PER SERVING

These veggie-filled burgers are great to have on hand so you can easily make a quick, nutritious meal. They can be stored in the refrigerator or frozen either before or after they are cooked.

- **2 slices whole wheat bread**
- **1¾ cups cooked or canned black beans, drained and rinsed**
- **½ cup rolled oats** (not instant)
- **¼ cup finely chopped carrot**
- **¼ cup finely chopped white button mushrooms**
- **¼ cup finely chopped onion**
- **2 tablespoons salsa, plus more if needed**
- **2 teaspoons nutritional yeast flakes**
- **2 garlic cloves, minced**
- **1 teaspoon ground cumin**
- **¼ teaspoon cayenne**
- **2 teaspoons vegetable oil**

Toast the bread lightly and tear it into medium-sized pieces. Put the pieces in a food processor and process into fine crumbs. Mash the beans in a large bowl with a fork or potato masher, leaving some chunks. Add the breadcrumbs, oats, carrot, mushrooms, onion, salsa, nutritional yeast flakes, garlic, cumin, and cayenne and mix with your hands or a fork until well combined. Add more salsa until the desired consistency is achieved.

Divide the mixture into 8 equal portions and form into thin patties. (Small patties are less likely to break apart.) Heat 1 teaspoon of the oil in a large skillet over medium heat. Put 4 of the patties in the skillet. Cook for 10 minutes, or until lightly browned on one side. Flip and continue cooking for 10 minutes, or until lightly browned on the other side. Transfer to a plate and cover to keep warm. Repeat with the remaining teaspoon of oil and the 4 remaining patties.

brilliant tofu BURGERS

$.75 PER SERVING   **MAKES 12 MEDIUM BURGERS** (6 SERVINGS)

Children and adults alike love these tofu burgers, which have a meatlike texture.

2 packages (14 ounces each) **lite firm silken tofu**

2½ cups rolled oats (not instant)

1½ tablespoons barbecue sauce or catsup (preferably sugar-free)

1½ tablespoons mustard seeds

1½ tablespoons low-sodium soy sauce

1½ tablespoons vegan worcestershire sauce or Bragg Liquid Aminos

Dash cayenne or hot pepper sauce

6 (6-inch) **whole-grain flour or corn tortillas**

6 romaine lettuce or spinach leaves

Preheat the oven to 350 degrees F.

Mash the tofu in a large bowl with a fork. Stir in the oats, barbecue sauce, mustard seeds, soy sauce, vegan worcestershire sauce, and cayenne and mix well.

Divide the mixture into 12 equal portions and form into thin patties. (Small patties are less likely to break apart.) Put the patties on a nonstick baking sheet or a stainless steel baking sheet misted with nonstick cooking spray. Bake the patties for 20 minutes. Flip and continue baking for another 10 minutes. Serve the burgers in the tortillas with the lettuce leaves.

TIPS

- These patties can be stored in the refrigerator for up to 3 days before cooking.
- Before reheating any leftovers, brush both sides of the burgers with your favorite stir-fry sauce.
- Add your favorite burger toppings, such as sliced onions and tomatoes.

cashew-and-sunflower seed BURGERS

MAKES 10 SERVINGS · **$.25** PER SERVING

Many of the vegetarian burgers that are sold in supermarkets are made with eggs. In this recipe, brown rice, cashews, and sunflower seeds bind the ingredients together, making eggs unnecessary. This recipe has no wheat or beans, making it gluten-free and bean-free.

> **3 cups water**
>
> **1½ cups brown rice**
>
> **½ cup unsalted roasted cashews**
>
> **¾ cups unsalted roasted sunflower seeds**
>
> **½ sweet onion, chopped**
>
> **3 carrots, chopped**
>
> **1 jalapeño chile, chopped** (optional)
>
> **1 tablespoon extra-virgin olive oil**
>
> **Salt**

Put the water in a medium saucepan and bring to a boil over high heat. Stir in the rice and return to a boil. Decrease the heat to low, cover, and cook for 45 minutes, or until the rice is tender and the water is absorbed.

Put the cashews and sunflower seeds in a food processor and process into a fine meal. Transfer to a large bowl. Put the onion, carrots, and optional chile in the food processor and process until finely shredded. Combine the onion mixture with the cashew mixture in the bowl and mix well. Add the rice and combine well with a fork or your hands.

Divide the mixture into 10 equal portions and form into thin patties. (Small patties are less likely to break apart.) Lightly coat a large skillet with 1½ teaspoons of the olive oil or lightly mist it with nonstick cooking spray. Put 5 of the patties in the skillet. Cook over medium heat for 6 to 8 minutes, or until lightly browned on one side. Flip and continue cooking for 6 to 8 minutes, or until lightly browned on the other side. Transfer to a plate and cover to keep warm. Add another 1½ teaspoons of the olive oil to the skillet or mist it again with nonstick cooking spray. Cook the 5 remaining patties for 6 to 8 minutes on each side. Pass salt at the table.

penny-pincher PITAS

$1.00 PER SERVING   **MAKES 4 SERVINGS**

When you want something hot and zesty for lunch, these pocket sandwiches fill the bill.

1 cup water

2 teaspoons vegetable broth powder

1 green onion, finely chopped

1¾ cups cooked or canned white, great northern, or cannellini beans, drained and rinsed

1 can (10 ounces) **diced tomatoes and chiles**

½ cup frozen corn

⅓ cup unsalted tomato paste

1 teaspoon chili powder

Hot pepper sauce

2 whole wheat pita breads, sliced in half

½ cup shredded lettuce

1 small tomato, chopped (about ½ cup)

¼ cup chopped cucumber

Put the water and vegetable broth powder in a medium skillet and bring to a boil over high heat. Decrease the heat to medium. Add the green onion and cook, stirring occasionally, for 5 minutes. Stir in the beans, tomatoes and chiles, corn, tomato paste, and chili powder. Cook, uncovered, for 10 minutes, stirring occasionally. Season with hot pepper sauce to taste. Spoon into the pita bread halves and top with the lettuce, tomato, and cucumber.

PORTOBELLO *poor boy sandwich*

MAKES 2 SERVINGS | **$2.00** PER SERVING

Here is a new take on the submarine sandwich that is flavorful and satisfying. You may want to cook extra mushrooms so you have leftovers for lunch the next day.

2 large portobello mushrooms, stemmed

¼ cup balsamic vinegar

2 to 4 tablespoons water

2 roasted red peppers, drained

2 ounces spinach leaves

1 small loaf whole wheat french bread, split lengthwise and halved crosswise

1 tablespoon low-sodium soy sauce (optional)

Put the mushrooms and vinegar in a medium bowl and marinate for about 20 minutes. Put the marinated mushrooms and 2 tablespoons of the water in a medium skillet and cook over medium heat for about 10 minutes, or until just softened and tender. As the mushrooms cook, add more water, if necessary, to prevent sticking, loosening them with a spatula. Top each mushroom with a roasted red pepper. Cover the skillet, decrease the heat to low, and cook for 3 to 5 minutes, or until the peppers are warmed through.

Divide the spinach leaves and put them on the 2 bottom pieces of the french bread. Cut the mushrooms and peppers in half and divide between the sandwiches. Sprinkle with the soy sauce, if desired, and top with the remaining pieces of bread.

calabacitas (BURRITO FILLING)

$.25 PER SERVING   **MAKES 10 SERVINGS**

This makes a wonderful side dish if you choose not to use it in a burrito. To "stretch" it, serve it on ten (10-inch) whole-grain flour tortillas. It's amazing how many children say they don't like vegetables. But I've never met a child yet who didn't love this vegetable-packed recipe.

1 small yellow onion, finely chopped

2 tablespoons water

2 small zucchini, quartered lengthwise and sliced

4 ounces white button mushrooms, sliced

½ teaspoon chili powder

½ teaspoon ground cumin

¼ cup frozen corn

Ground pepper

Put the onion and 1 tablespoon of the water in a large skillet over medium-high heat and cook and stir until the water has evaporated. Stir in the remaining 1 tablespoon of the water, the zucchini, and mushrooms, cover, and cook for 10 minutes, or until the zucchini and mushrooms have released their juices. Decrease the heat to low. Stir in the chili powder and cumin, cover, and cook for 5 minutes, or until the mushrooms are soft. Stir in the corn and cook for 5 minutes to heat through. Season with pepper to taste.

TIP: Children love to be involved in creating their meals. They can build their own burritos when you serve Calabacitas with small bowls of condiments, such as avocado slices, vegan cheese, sliced olives, parsley sprigs, salsa, and chopped tomatoes.

load-'em-up BURRITOS

MAKES 8 TO 10 SERVINGS **$1.25** PER SERVING

Dinners are happy occasions when kids feel that they have control over what they eat. Like Calabacitas (page 90), this recipe works well when served with small bowls of condiments. The ingredients are not set in stone, so include any nutritious toppings that the kids request.

1½ cups cooked or canned kidney beans, drained and rinsed

1 can (6 ounces) unsalted tomato paste

10 (10-inch) whole-grain flour tortillas

10 (6-inch) corn tortillas

1 tablespoon water

12 ounces white button mushrooms, thinly sliced

1 sweet onion, chopped

4 large carrots, shredded

2 cups shredded romaine lettuce

1 can (6 ounces) small olives, drained and sliced

1 to 2 tomatoes, chopped

1 avocado, diced (optional)

4 ounces alfalfa sprouts (optional)

½ cup raw sunflower seeds (optional)

3 radishes, sliced or shredded (optional)

Preheat the oven to 350 degrees F.

Put the beans and tomato paste in a food processor and pulse for 2 to 3 minutes, or until smooth. Alternatively, put the beans in a medium bowl, mash them thoroughly with a fork, and stir in the tomato paste until well mixed. Put the whole-grain flour tortillas in a large glass baking dish, and put the corn tortillas in a separate large glass baking dish. Allow the tortillas to curl a little so that they fit. Spread some of the bean mixture on top of each tortilla to make burritos and bake for 5 to 10 minutes, or until the tortillas are toasty and just golden around the edges.

While the burritos are baking, put the water in a small skillet over medium heat. Add the mushrooms and onion, keeping them separated, and cook over medium heat for 10 minutes, adding more water as it evaporates, 1 tablespoon at a time, until the onion is translucent.

Arrange the mushrooms, onion, carrots, lettuce, olives, tomatoes, and the optional avocado, alfalfa sprouts, sunflower seeds, and radishes in separate piles on a large platter or in individual serving bowls. Serve the burritos with the toppings on the side.

TIP: Canned refried beans are often too salty. I like to make my own low-salt version by mixing beans and unsalted tomato paste in a food processor.

tasty TACOS

It is difficult to find taco shells that are low in fat and aren't deep-fried. That's why this recipe calls for making your own taco shells with corn tortillas, which can be very affordable when sold in large quantities at big-box stores. If you feel like splurging a little, try refrigerated or frozen sprouted tortillas, which can be tastier.

1¾ **cups cooked or canned pinto beans, drained and rinsed**

6 **tablespoons salsa, plus more for garnish**

¼ **cup water**

4 (6-inch) **corn tortillas**

2 **cups romaine or other lettuce, shredded**

2 **tomatoes, chopped**

½ **avocado, chopped** (optional)

2 **green onions, sliced**

Combine the beans and salsa in a medium bowl, mashing the mixture with a fork or potato masher until slightly chunky. Put the bean mixture and water in a small saucepan and cook and stir over medium heat for about 5 minutes, or just until warmed through. Put the tortillas, one at a time, in a small, dry skillet and cook over medium heat, flipping from one side to the other about every 10 seconds, or until soft. Transfer the tortillas to plates, spread ¼ of the bean mixture on each tortilla, and top with the lettuce, tomato, optional avocado, and green onions. Garnish with additional salsa or pass it at the table.

TIPS

- Substitute 1 can (15 ounces) of fat-free vegetarian refried beans for the pinto beans, although they are higher in sodium and more expensive.
- Instead of mashing them by hand, process the beans and salsa in a food processor for 1 to 2 minutes, or until smooth and creamy.
- Instead of heating the bean mixture on the stove, put it in a microwave-safe bowl and heat it in the microwave for 1 minute.

QUESADILLAS *with not-so-refried beans*

MAKES 4 SERVINGS   **$2.00** PER SERVING

Quesadillas are fun to eat with your hands and make a flavorful, quick, and inexpensive lunch or dinner.

> **2 small red onions, finely chopped**
>
> **1 can** (6 ounces) **pitted black olives, thinly sliced**
>
> **1 avocado, finely chopped**
>
> **1 small red bell pepper, chopped**
>
> **⅓ cup chopped fresh cilantro**
>
> **1½ tablespoons freshly squeezed lime juice**
>
> **4** (6-inch) **whole-grain flour tortillas**
>
> **1¾ cups cooked or canned pinto beans, drained and rinsed**
>
> **2 tablespoons salsa**

Preheat the broiler.

Put the onions, olives, avocado, bell pepper, cilantro, and lime juice in a medium bowl and stir to combine.

Mist a large baking sheet with nonstick cooking spray and place the tortillas on the sheet. Mist the tops of the tortillas lightly with nonstick cooking spray. Broil 2 to 4 inches from the heat source for about 45 seconds, or until lightly browned. Turn the tortillas over and broil the other side for about 45 seconds, or until lightly browned.

Put the beans and salsa in a medium bowl and mix well, mashing the bean mixture with a fork if you prefer a smoother texture. Divide the bean mixture into 4 portions and spread 1 portion on each of the tortillas, taking care not to break them. Divide the onion mixture into 4 portions and spread 1 portion on top of the bean mixture on each of the tortillas. Cut each tortilla into 4 wedges and serve immediately.

TIPS

- If you can splurge a little for sprouted whole-grain tortillas, especially ones that are freshly made, you'll love this recipe even more.
- When spraying the tortillas with nonstick cooking spray, hold the spray bottle back far enough so that the oil reaching the tortillas is a fine mist. If you don't have cooking spray, coat the baking sheet with 1 tablespoon of vegetable oil before placing the tortillas on the sheet. Oiling the tops of the tortillas isn't necessary; it just provides more crunch.

COUSCOUS AND BEANS

$.75 PER SERVING   **MAKES 10 SERVINGS**

It's a question that vegans hear all the time: "Where do you get your protein?" Next time someone asks you this question, invite him over for this delightful dinner.

1½ **cups whole wheat couscous**

2 **cups boiling water**

3 **cups cooked or canned garbanzo beans, drained and rinsed**

1 **cup finely shredded purple or green cabbage or a combination**

½ **red or green bell pepper, chopped**

½ **cup chopped fresh parsley**

½ **cup golden raisins**

1 **carrot, grated**

3 **green onions, finely chopped**

2 **tablespoons freshly squeezed lemon juice**

1 **tablespoon extra-virgin olive oil** (optional)

Salt

⅛ **to** ¼ **teaspoon curry powder or ground turmeric** (optional)

Put the couscous in a large heatproof bowl, add the boiling water, stir, and cover. Let sit for 5 to 10 minutes, or until all the water has been absorbed. Fluff with a fork. Stir in the beans, cabbage, bell pepper, parsley, raisins, carrot, and green onions. Mix the lemon juice, optional oil, and salt to taste in a small bowl. Pour the lemon mixture over the couscous mixture, add the optional curry powder, and toss to mix.

Serve at room temperature or chilled.

TIPS

- Add slivered almonds, sesame seeds, or sunflower seeds as a topping if you want more crunch and more protein.
- If you like, substitute cooked quinoa for the couscous.

PENNE *for pennies*

MAKES 8 SERVINGS   **$1.00** PER SERVING

Who wants to pay for a high-priced pasta dish at a restaurant when pasta is so easy to make at home? This recipe, which features Asian flavors, is a departure from traditional pasta dishes.

BROCCOLI AND PENNE

1 large head broccoli, chopped

12 ounces whole wheat penne pasta

3 tablespoons Ginger-Soy Vinaigrette

1 package (8 ounces) **thai- or teriyaki-style baked tofu, cut into 1-inch cubes**

GINGER-SOY VINAIGRETTE

1¼ cup rice vinegar

¼ cup minced shallots or onion

2 tablespoons chopped fresh ginger

2 tablespoons low-sodium soy sauce

½ teaspoon toasted sesame oil

1 garlic clove

Hot pepper sauce

½ cup water

¼ cup unsalted roasted cashews

To make the broccoli and penne, fill a large pot with water and bring to a boil over high heat. Add the broccoli and cook for 3 to 4 minutes, or until tender yet firm. Using a slotted spoon, transfer the broccoli to a large plate and set aside. Return the water to a boil, add the pasta, and cook for 7 to 8 minutes, or until al dente. Drain the pasta in a colander.

To make the vinaigrette, combine the vinegar, shallots, ginger, soy sauce, oil, garlic, and hot pepper sauce to taste in a blender and process until smooth. Add the water and cashews and process until smooth. Transfer the vinaigrette to a large skillet. Add the broccoli and tofu and cook over medium heat, tossing gently, for 1 to 2 minutes, or until heated through. Put the pasta in a large serving bowl, add the broccoli mixture, and toss gently until evenly distributed.

cabbage WRAPS

$2.50 PER SERVING | **MAKES 2 SERVINGS**

Cabbage, a member of the cruciferous family of vegetables, is known for its ability to fight cancer. Sometimes it's a challenge to fit this nutrition superstar into your diet, but this recipe makes it easy.

CABBAGE WRAPS	TAHINI DRESSING
1 head green cabbage	**½ cup tahini**
2 carrots, finely grated	**½ cup water**
½ large beet, grated	**2 tablespoons freshly squeezed lemon juice**
½ cup clover, broccoli, or alfalfa sprouts	**2 teaspoons cider vinegar**
	¼ teaspoon salt (optional)
	⅛ teaspoon ground pepper (optional)

To make the cabbage wraps, remove the stem from the cabbage and discard the outer leaves. Cut the head of cabbage in half lengthwise and remove 4 of the outer leaves, being careful not to tear them. Using a mandoline or sharp knife, thinly slice the remaining cabbage until you have about 2 cups. Put ½ cup of the sliced cabbage and one-quarter of the carrots, beets, and sprouts into each of the 4 leaves to make 4 wraps.

To make the tahini dressing, put all the ingredients in a blender or food processor and process until smooth. If the dressing is too thick, add more water, 1 teaspoon at a time, until the desired consistency is achieved. Spoon 1 tablespoon of the dressing over the filling in each of the wraps. Fold each wrap in half and serve.

TIPS

- It is not necessary to peel the carrots. In addition, if the beet skins are thin, they don't need to be peeled either. Thicker-skinned beets can taste bitter to some people, so you may have to experiment.

- Be sure to eat the wraps over a bowl or a plate since the beets will release their juices.

- These wraps can be made with cooked beets and carrots, but they are faster to prepare and taste fresher with raw vegetables.

VEGGIES *in a blanket*

MAKES 2 SERVINGS   **$1.50** PER SERVING

For my money, this recipe, which is very easy to make, can be a main course at lunch or dinner any day.

¼ **cup vegan cream cheese or Hummus** (page 103)

4 (10-inch) **whole-grain flour tortillas**

1 **carrot, grated**

4 **lettuce leaves,** ½ **to 1 cup baby spinach leaves, or** ½ **cup alfalfa or broccoli sprouts, or a combination**

Spread 1 tablespoon of the vegan cream cheese on each tortilla. Top with the carrot and lettuce. Roll up each tortilla tightly and serve.

TIPS

- Many natural food stores and some local bakeries sell fresh sprouted-grain tortillas or burrito shells. If you can't find those, the frozen sprouted varieties are delicious too. Look for low-fat or no-fat varieties.

- These rolls make an attractive appetizer. Fasten each roll with three toothpicks spaced an equal distance apart. Cut the roll between each toothpick to make four 1-inch pieces.

VEGGIE *sushi*

$.75 PER SERVING   **MAKES 6 SERVINGS**

25¢ 25¢ 25¢

Making sushi is really very easy once you get the hang of it. You'll need a bamboo sushi mat for this recipe.

2 cups water

1 cup medium-grain brown rice

1 tablespoon agave nectar or sugar

1 tablespoon rice vinegar

1 carrot, sliced into matchsticks

3 ounces fresh shiitake mushrooms, stemmed and diced

2 tablespoons unsalted roasted sesame seeds

½ cucumber, peeled, seeded, and sliced into matchsticks

1 teaspoon freshly squeezed lime juice

6 sheets toasted nori

1 avocado, thinly sliced

Put the water in a medium saucepan and bring to a boil over high heat. Stir in the rice and return to a boil. Decrease the heat to low, cover, and cook for 45 minutes, or until the rice is tender and the water is absorbed. Remove from the heat, keep covered, and let sit for 10 minutes. Fluff with a fork and transfer to a large bowl.

Whisk the agave nectar and vinegar with a fork to blend. Stir into the rice with a fork.

Place a steamer basket in a large saucepan, add 1 inch of water, and bring to a boil over high heat. Put the carrot and mushrooms in the steamer, cover, and steam for about 3 minutes, or until tender. Transfer the carrot and mushrooms to a large bowl. Add the sesame seeds, stir to combine, and let cool. When the vegetable mixture has cooled, add the cucumber and lime juice and gently stir to combine.

Place a sushi mat on a flat, clean surface and set a small bowl of water nearby. Put 1 nori sheet on top of the mat. Put a spoonful of rice (about one-sixth of the rice) on the nori sheet and use the spoon to press the rice firmly into an even layer, leaving a ¼-inch border around the edges. Arrange about one-sixth of the carrot mixture in a line on the lower third of the nori sheet and place 2 or 3 slices of avocado on top. Using the sushi mat, carefully roll the sushi into a log. When you are finished, dip a finger in the bowl of water and wet the underside of the top edge of the nori. Seal the edge shut by running a dry finger along the top side of the wet edge. As long as the roll isn't overstuffed, it should stay sealed. Carefully remove the mat and place the finished roll on a cutting board. Cut the roll into 5 or 6 pieces with a sharp knife, rinsing the knife with water between cuts. Repeat the process with the remaining nori sheets and filling.

TIPS

- If you haven't used a sushi mat before, it may take a few tries until you're happy with their appearance. Even if they don't look perfect, practice rolls will taste just as delicious.

- Try adding some radish sprouts to the filling to give the rolls a splash of vibrant green. Or try using other ingredients, such as shredded cabbage, summer squash, or zucchini or sliced asparagus, green onions, roasted red peppers, or tofu. The possibilities are endless.

- Serve the sushi with pickled ginger, low-sodium soy sauce, and wasabi.

penny wise
spreads
and sides

SPREADS

guacamole PLUS

$.50 PER SERVING   **MAKES 8 SERVINGS**

My students love to serve this recipe at parties and potluck dinners. They tell me no one ever guesses that this tasty appetizer has peas in it!

1 avocado

1 cup frozen green peas, thawed, or canned peas, drained and rinsed

½ cup salsa

1 green onion, minced (optional)

1 tablespoon chopped fresh cilantro (optional)

2 teaspoons freshly squeezed lemon juice

1 teaspoon ground cumin

8 whole wheat pita breads, sliced into wedges, or assorted raw vegetables, sliced

Put the avocado flesh and peas in a food processor and process until smooth. Add the salsa, optional green onion, and cilantro, lemon juice, and cumin. Continue to process until smooth. Spoon into a serving dish and serve with the pita wedges.

TIPS

- For a chunkier texture, mash the ingredients in a large bowl with a fork instead of using a food processor.
- Instead of serving Guacamole Plus as an appetizer, use it as a flavorful condiment in burritos or tacos.

hummus

$.75 PER SERVING

This popular staple stores well in the refrigerator and makes a quick, filling snack when hunger strikes.

3½ cups cooked or canned garbanzo beans, drained (reserve liquid), and rinsed

6 green onions (optional)

2 tablespoons tahini

1 to 2 garlic cloves

½ teaspoon freshly squeezed lemon juice

¼ teaspoon ground cumin

¼ teaspoon ground black pepper

8 whole wheat pita breads, sliced into wedges, or assorted raw vegetables, sliced

Put the beans, about ½ cup of the bean liquid, optional green onions, tahini, garlic, lemon juice, cumin, and pepper in a blender or food processor and process until smooth. Add more of the bean liquid if a smoother consistency is desired. To serve, spread on the pita bread or use as a dip.

TIP: To cut down on fat and cost, replace the tahini with an equal amount of bean liquid or water. The hummus will be thinner and have a chunkier texture.

ROASTED RED PEPPER HUMMUS: Process 1 cup of drained roasted red peppers with the garbanzo beans and other ingredients.

thai NO-FRY *spring rolls*

25¢ 25¢ 25¢ 25¢ **$1.00** PER SERVING · **MAKES 4 SERVINGS**

Spring rolls taste so much better when they are not deep-fried. They also are so much cheaper when you make them at home. Here, tender rice paper wrappers contain a fresh filling, and the rolls are accented by a sweet-and-spicy dipping sauce.

SPRING ROLLS

8 large rice paper wrappers
(about 8½ inches in diameter)

½ cup shredded napa cabbage

½ cup shredded romaine lettuce

1 carrot, shredded

¼ cup chopped fresh basil

4 teaspoons chopped fresh mint

DIPPING SAUCE

¼ cup low-sodium soy sauce

2 tablespoons unsalted natural creamy peanut butter

1 tablespoon rice vinegar

1 teaspoon freshly squeezed lime juice

1 green onion, thinly sliced

1 tablespoon chopped fresh cilantro

1 teaspoon grated fresh ginger

Pinch cayenne

To make the spring rolls, pour warm water into a large, shallow bowl until it is half full. Soften each rice paper wrapper, one at a time, just until pliable, by briefly immersing it in the warm water. (Do not allow the wrapper to absorb too much water or it will be difficult to work with.) Transfer the wrapper to a plate. Arrange about 1 tablespoon each of the cabbage, lettuce, and carrot and a pinch of the basil and mint in the lower third of the wrapper. Carefully fold the bottom edge of the wrapper over the filling. Fold in the sides and continue rolling up from the bottom. Place on a platter, seam-side down. Repeat the process with each of the remaining wrappers.

To make the dipping sauce, combine the soy sauce, peanut butter, vinegar, and lime juice in a medium bowl and mix well with a fork. Stir in the green onion, cilantro, ginger, and cayenne and mix well. Serve the spring rolls with the dipping sauce on the side.

TIP: Leftover dipping sauce would taste great on udon noodles, which can be found at any natural food store.

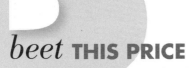

beet THIS PRICE

Many people don't know that you can eat beet greens. Beet bulbs, the red parts, are very sweet, and many children love them, if given a chance to eat them.

> **4 beets, scrubbed and trimmed**
>
> **beet greens from 4 beets, stemmed and chopped**
>
> **2 tablespoons water**
>
> **3 tablespoons agave nectar or maple syrup**
>
> **Cider vinegar**
>
> **¼ cup raisins**

Steam the beets in a steamer basket over simmering water for 45 to 60 minutes, until tender or a paring knife can be easily inserted. Let the beets cool slightly, then slip off their skins and cut them into bite-sized chunks.

While the beets cool, put the greens in a medium saucepan, add the water, cover, and cook over medium-low heat for 10 minutes, or until tender. Transfer the greens to a serving bowl and drizzle with half of the agave nectar and vinegar to taste. Add the beets, drizzle with the remaining agave nectar, and sprinkle with the raisins.

wok-sautéed GREENS

Making this recipe when the greens are in season will take a big bite out of the recipe cost.

¼ **cup finely chopped green onions**

2 **garlic cloves, minced**

1½ **teaspoons low-sodium soy sauce**

½ **teaspoon vegan chili paste**

¼ **cup water, plus more if needed**

¼ **cup water chestnuts, finely chopped**

1 **small yellow onion, finely chopped**

1 **carrot, finely chopped**

1 **tablespoon freshly squeezed lime juice**

1 **bunch mizuna, spinach, or other tender greens, stemmed**

Combine the green onions, garlic, soy sauce, and vegan chili paste in a small bowl. Put the water, water chestnuts, yellow onion, and carrot in a wok or large skillet over medium-high heat and cook, stirring constantly, until the vegetables are softened and the onion is translucent. Add more water, 1 tablespoon at a time, if needed to keep the contents from sticking to the wok. Add the green onion mixture, lime juice, and mizuna and cook, stirring frequently, just until the greens are slightly wilted.

TIP: If time permits, cover and refrigerate the green onion mixture for 1 hour before using, to meld the flavors.

BRAISED *collards or kale*

The combination of soy and balsamic vinegar neutralizes any bitterness in the dark leafy greens. I wish I had a nickel for every person in my cooking classes who said, "Wow, I never tasted collards or kale before, and this is so good!"

2 garlic cloves, minced

¼ cup water

1 bunch collard greens or kale, stemmed and chopped

2 teaspoons low-sodium soy sauce

1 teaspoon balsamic vinegar

Mist a large skillet or wok with nonstick cooking spray. Put the garlic in the skillet and cook and stir over medium heat for 1 to 2 minutes, or until the garlic is translucent. Add 1 or 2 teaspoons of the water if the garlic sticks to the skillet. Add the greens, remaining water, soy sauce, and vinegar, cover, and cook for 10 minutes, or until the greens are wilted and tender.

TIPS

- Greens are fresher and less expensive when purchased in bunches rather than prechopped in bags.
- To quickly and neatly chop large amounts of greens, remove the stems, stack the leaves in a pile, roll them up, and slice them into thin strips.

ratatouille

25¢ 25¢ 25¢ | **$.75** PER SERVING | **MAKES 8 SERVINGS**

In late summer, when eggplant is in season, a big batch of ratatouille can be made for pennies. Leftovers taste great.

3 cups water

1 tablespoon salt

1 large eggplant, cut into bite-sized chunks

2 small onions, chopped

2 celery stalks, chopped

6 garlic cloves, minced

6 to 8 tomatoes, chopped, or 1 can (14.5 ounces) **unsalted diced tomatoes, undrained**

8 ounces cremini or white button mushrooms, sliced

1 teaspoon italian seasoning

½ teaspoon ground black pepper

½ teaspoon dried thyme

Pour 2 cups of the water into a large bowl, add the salt, and stir to dissolve. Add the eggplant. (If necessary, add additional water to cover the eggplant.) Soak for 10 minutes. Drain, rinse, and drain again.

Put the onions, celery, garlic, and ¼ cup of the remaining water in a large saucepan over medium heat and cook for about 10 minutes, or until the vegetables are soft. Add the eggplant and another ¼ cup of the water. Cook, stirring occasionally, for 8 to 10 minutes, or until the eggplant is soft. Add more water, if necessary, to keep the mixture from drying out or sticking to the pan. Stir in the tomatoes, mushrooms, italian seasoning, pepper, and thyme. Cover and cook, stirring occasionally, for 10 minutes.

TIPS

- Ratatouille is filling served alone or over pasta shells, brown rice, or another whole grain.
- Before serving, sprinkle shredded vegan cheese on top of the hot ratatouille so that it melts.

sweet potato SKINS

MAKES 4 SERVINGS　　　　　　　　　　　　　**$1.50** PER SERVING

This fragrantly spiced dish looks and tastes like the popular restaurant appetizer, just without the high price tag and excess fat.

> **2 sweet potatoes, scrubbed**
>
> **4 ounces vegan cheese, shredded**
>
> **½ cup walnuts, chopped**
>
> **2 garlic cloves, minced**
>
> **3 tablespoons chopped fresh parsley**
>
> **1 tablespoon olive oil**
>
> **½ teaspoon dried oregano**
>
> **½ teaspoon dried rosemary**
>
> **½ teaspoon dried sage**
>
> **½ teaspoon dried thyme**
>
> **Salt**
>
> **Ground pepper**
>
> **2 green onions, thinly sliced**

Preheat the oven to 400 degrees F.

Put the sweet potatoes on a baking sheet and bake for 35 to 45 minutes, or until tender but not mushy.

While the sweet potatoes bake, combine the vegan cheese, half the walnuts, and the garlic in a small bowl. Combine the parsley, oil, oregano, rosemary, sage, thyme, and salt and pepper to taste in a separate small bowl.

Remove the sweet potatoes from the oven but do not turn off the oven. Cut the sweet potatoes in half lengthwise and scoop out the flesh, leaving a ¼-inch lining of potato flesh in the skins. Arrange the sweet potato skins on the baking sheet. (Reserve the scooped-out flesh for another use.)

Fill the sweet potato skins with the cheese mixture and bake for 5 to 10 minutes, or until almost crisp. Remove from the oven and sprinkle with the parsley mixture. Change the oven setting to broil and broil the sweet potatoes for 4 to 6 minutes, or until browned in parts and piping hot. Sprinkle with the green onions and remaining walnuts. Serve hot.

polenta

LESS THAN $.25 PER SERVING **MAKES 4 SERVINGS**

This delicious, creamy grain can be served at breakfast, lunch, or dinner. Known as "grits" in some parts of the country, polenta is coarsely ground cornmeal. It is available in different colors and grinds and takes little time to prepare.

3 cups water

1 cup coarse-grind cornmeal or grits

2 teaspoons salt (optional)

Pour the water into a small saucepan and bring to a boil over high heat. Very slowly whisk in the cornmeal. Stir in the salt, if using. Decrease the heat to medium-low, cover, and cook, stirring frequently, for 5 to 10 minutes, or until very thick.

TIP: This is one of the most striking examples of how it pays to make your own instead of buying a prepared version, as tempting as the latter may seem. One serving of polenta made from a five-pound bag of cornmeal costs about a nickel. But the same half-cup serving from a tube of premade polenta (often found in the refrigerated section of grocery stores) costs about $.75, or fifteen times as much!

VARIATION: Put the cooked cornmeal in a loaf pan and chill for 2 hours. Slice and serve as desired. If serving for breakfast, sprinkle with raisins or fresh berries.

POTATO *pancakes*

Potato pancakes are wonderful any time of year, but they truly appeal when the temperature drops. In addition, they are so much more nutritious than french fries.

2 large sweet potatoes, or 4 yukon gold potatoes, unpeeled

2 large carrots

2 small yellow onions

6 tablespoons all-purpose whole wheat flour or whole wheat pastry flour

Salt

Ground pepper

Shred the potatoes, carrots, and onions in a food processor. Alternatively, use a manual shredder or mandoline. Transfer the shredded vegetables to a large bowl. Add the flour and salt and pepper to taste. Mix with a rubber spatula until evenly combined. Gently form the mixture into 4 to 8 small ¼-inch-thick patties.

Mist a large skillet with nonstick cooking spray over medium heat. Arrange the potato patties in the skillet and press down on them lightly with a spatula. Cook for 10 minutes, or until lightly browned on one side. Flip the patties over and cook for 10 minutes longer, or until lightly browned on the other side. Serve hot.

TIPS

- Put the shredded potatoes in a bowl of cold water to prevent them from turning brown. Drain well before using.

- Small, thin patties will cook faster and more evenly than large, thick patties.

wheat berry PILAF

$.75 PER SERVING   **MAKES 6 SERVINGS**

There's nothing quite like the sweet crunchiness of wheat berries. They're a fantastic source of fiber too.

2 cups wheat berries, soaked, drained, and rinsed (see tip)

¼ cup freshly squeezed orange juice

1½ tablespoons freshly squeezed lemon juice

1½ teaspoons flaxseed oil or canola oil

Salt

Ground pepper

2 small beets, peeled and grated

1 small bunch green onions, thinly sliced

¾ cup raisins

1 carrot, grated

Put the wheat berries in a large saucepan with several inches of water. Cover and bring to a boil over high heat. Decrease the heat to medium-low and cook, still covered, for 1 hour, or until the wheat berries are tender and some break open. Drain well and set aside to cool.

Whisk the orange juice, lemon juice, oil, and salt and pepper to taste in a small bowl. Pour over the wheat berries and toss to coat. Add the beets, green onions, raisins, and carrot and toss again to coat. Serve at room temperature or chilled.

TIP: Put the wheat berries in a large bowl and cover with several inches of cold water. Soak for 8 to 12 hours. Drain and rinse the wheat berries before proceeding with the recipe.

no remorse *desserts* *and snacks*

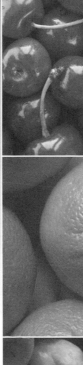

113

apple CRISP

$1.00 PER SERVING   **MAKES 2 SERVINGS**

This version is every bit as good as Mom's. Whole-grain flour adds even more fiber.

4 large medjool dates, pitted and chopped

¼ cup rolled oats

¼ cup all-purpose whole wheat or rye flour

2 teaspoons raisins

1 teaspoon ground cinnamon

2 medium apples

Combine the dates, oats, flour, raisins, and cinnamon in a small bowl. Remove the apple cores to within ¼ inch of the bottom of each apple. Put about 1 inch of water into a medium saucepan and then put the apples in the saucepan. Stuff each apple with as much of the date mixture as possible, allowing each one to overflow. Cover and cook over medium heat for 20 to 25 minutes, or until tender. Serve hot, warm, or chilled.

TIP: Alternatively, the apples can be baked. Preheat the oven to 350 degrees F, arrange the apples in an uncovered baking dish, and bake for 30 to 40 minutes, until soft.

BERRY *pudding*

$1.00 PER SERVING

This dessert is decadent without the guilt. Pure and simple.

2¾ cups frozen unsweetened berries of choice, thawed

1 package (12 ounces) **reduced-fat extra-firm silken tofu, crumbled**

2 tablespoons agave nectar, 3 tablespoons sugar, or 1 tablespoon berry liqueur

Combine all the ingredients in a blender or food processor and process until smooth. Spoon into four pudding dishes and refrigerate until chilled.

blueberry tortilla PIZZA

$1.50 PER SERVING   **MAKES 4 SERVINGS**

This is a much more healthful version of French crêpes, which are traditionally made with eggs and butter.

1 package (12 ounces) **firm or extra-firm silken tofu**

2 teaspoons cinnamon sugar

1 pint fresh blueberries

½ cup sliced strawberries

1 tablespoon nonhydrogenated vegan margarine

4 (10-inch) **whole-grain flour tortillas**

¼ cup unsweetened flaked coconut (optional)

Preheat the broiler.

Mash the tofu with a fork in a small bowl. Stir in 1 teaspoon of the cinnamon sugar. Combine the blueberries and strawberries in another small bowl. Put the vegan margarine in a microwave-safe bowl and heat in the microwave for 10 seconds, or until melted.

Arrange the tortillas on a broiler pan and brush lightly and sparingly with the margarine. Sprinkle with the remaining cinnamon sugar. Broil about 6 inches from the heat source for about 3 minutes, or until lightly browned, taking care not to burn. Remove from the oven, let cool slightly, and transfer to plates. Spread the tofu mixture on the tortillas and top with the blueberry mixture. Sprinkle with the coconut, if desired.

TIPS

- Try to get lite silken tofu, which has less fat. However, either lite or regular silken tofu will work in this recipe.

- To make cinnamon sugar, combine 2 teaspoons of sugar with ½ teaspoon of ground cinnamon in a small bowl or measuring cup.

chocolate surprise CAKE

Here's a clever way to get children to eat their vegetables. They won't even detect the beets, carrots, and zucchini in this chocolate cake.

CHOCOLATE CAKE

1⅔ cups whole wheat pastry flour,
or 1 cup unbleached white flour and
⅔ cup all-purpose whole wheat flour

3 tablespoons unsweetened cocoa powder

1 tablespoon baking soda

1 teaspoon baking powder

3 cups whole pitted dates

1 can (8 ounces) pineapple chunks, packed
in juice, drained

1 cup unsweetened applesauce

1 banana

1 cup shredded beets

1 cup chopped walnuts

¾ cup shredded carrots

½ cup coarsely chopped dates

½ cup currants (optional)

½ cup shredded zucchini

1 cup vanilla soymilk

1 teaspoon vanilla extract

CHOCOLATE ICING

1 cup unsalted raw macadamia nuts
or cashews

½ cup raw brazil nuts or hazelnuts

1 cup vanilla soymilk

⅔ cup whole pitted dates

2 tablespoons unsweetened cocoa powder

1 teaspoon vanilla extract

Preheat the oven to 350 degrees F.

To make the cake, put the flour, cocoa powder, baking soda, and baking powder in a medium bowl and stir with a dry whisk until well combined. Put the whole dates, the pineapple, applesauce, and banana in a blender and process until smooth.

Combine the beets, walnuts, carrots, chopped dates, optional currants, and zucchini in a large bowl. Stir in the flour mixture, soymilk, and vanilla extract. Add the blended date mixture and mix well.

Pour the batter into a 9 x 13-inch nonstick baking pan or two 9-inch round nonstick cake pans. Bake for 1 hour, or until a knife inserted into the center comes out clean. Cool in the pan on a rack for 10 minutes. Remove from the pan and transfer to a serving platter.

To make the icing, put all the icing ingredients in a blender and process until smooth and creamy. Spread over the warm or cooled cake.

TIP: Because this cake batter is exceptionally moist, the one-hour baking time, which is longer than necessary for most cakes, is needed here.

carrot cake **TO LIVE FOR**

$1.00 PER SERVING	**MAKES 10 SERVINGS**

This cake contains no fat and is sweet even without the icing. However, the optional icing, which does contain fat, can transform this carrot cake into a very respectable homemade birthday cake. It was my kids' favorite birthday cake for many years.

CARROT CAKE

2 cups finely grated carrots, packed

1¾ cups water

1½ cups brown sugar, packed

1 cup raisins or other chopped dried fruit

1 teaspoon vanilla extract

3 cups all-purpose whole wheat flour

2 teaspoons baking powder

1 teaspoon baking soda

1 teaspoon ground cinnamon

1 teaspoon salt

½ teaspoon ground ginger

½ teaspoon freshly grated nutmeg

¼ teaspoon ground cloves

ICING (OPTIONAL)

1 package (8 ounces) **vegan cream cheese**

⅓ cup nonhydrogenated vegan margarine, softened

2 cups confectioners' sugar

1 teaspoon vanilla extract

To make the cake, combine the carrots, water, brown sugar, raisins, and vanilla extract in a medium saucepan and bring to a boil over high heat. Decrease the heat to low and cook, stirring occasionally, for 5 minutes. Remove from the heat, cover, and let sit for at least 1 hour.

Preheat the oven to 300 degrees F. Lightly oil or spray and flour a 9 x 13-inch glass baking dish.

Put the flour, baking powder, baking soda, cinnamon, salt, ginger, nutmeg, and cloves in a large bowl and stir with a dry whisk until well combined. Stir the cooled carrot mixture into the flour mixture just until no flour remains on the sides of the bowl. Pour into the prepared baking dish and bake for about 1 hour, or until the cake feels firm to the touch and a knife inserted into the center comes out clean.

Cool in the baking dish on a rack for 10 minutes. Put a large serving plate over the baking dish and carefully turn the plate and baking dish over together. Carefully lift the baking dish straight up to release the cake.

To make the optional icing, put the vegan cream cheese and margarine in a medium bowl and beat with an electric mixer until well combined. Beat in the sugar and vanilla extract until smooth. Spread over the warm cake.

APRICOT *has a date*

This sweet, chewy confection tastes like an indulgence. However, the fiber and protein make it a sensible treat.

> **1 fresh apricot, chopped**
>
> **¼ cup finely chopped dried apricots**
>
> **¼ cup finely chopped raw cashews**
>
> **¼ cup finely chopped dates, preferably medjool**
>
> **¼ cup finely chopped dried figs**
>
> **¼ cup raisins, dark or light currants, or a mixture of the two**
>
> **¼ cup unsalted creamy natural peanut butter or nut butter of choice**
>
> **2 tablespoons unsweetened cocoa powder**

Put the fresh apricot, dried apricots, cashews, dates, figs, and raisins in a large bowl. Add the peanut butter and mix thoroughly with a fork. Roll into bite-sized balls, put the balls on a plate, and sprinkle them with the cocoa powder.

TIPS

- Experiment with different fruits and nuts, depending on what is in season or available.
- Carob (a plant-based chocolate substitute) may be used instead of cocoa powder, but it is more expensive.
- Cashew pieces are $1 to $2 cheaper per pound than whole cashews. There is no need to buy whole cashews for recipes that call for chopped nuts.

grapefruit-berry SORBET

$.75 PER SERVING MAKES 4 SERVINGS

This sherbet has a beautiful rosy color and is naturally sweet.

2 cups red grapefruit sections

1 (10-ounce) **package frozen sliced strawberries**

¼ **to** ½ **cup soymilk**

Place the grapefruit sections in a single layer on a baking sheet and freeze until firm. Put the frozen grapefruit, frozen strawberries, and ¼ cup of the soymilk in a blender or food processor and process with short pulses until the fruit is finely chopped. Add more soymilk and pulse until the mixture is smooth and creamy. Spoon into parfait dishes and serve immediately, or transfer to a freezer container and store in the freezer.

TIP: Grapefruit-Berry Sorbet is most affordable when the strawberries and grape-fruit are in season.

chocolate MOUSSE

MAKES 8 SERVINGS　　　　　　　　　　**$.50** PER SERVING

This is a guilt-free version of the high-fat, high-calorie French dessert. Your guests will be amazed when you tell them this mousse is made without heavy cream or any other dairy products.

1 cup semisweet nondairy chocolate chips

1½ cup vanilla soymilk

1 package (12 ounces) **low-fat or no-fat firm or extra-firm silken tofu**

⅓ cup maple syrup (optional)

½ teaspoon vanilla extract

Put the chocolate chips and soymilk in a microwave-safe bowl and heat in the microwave for 1 minute. Alternatively, warm the chocolate chips and soymilk in a small saucepan on medium heat for 5 minutes, or until the chocolate chips are just shiny. Let the mixture sit for 2 minutes, then transfer to a blender or food processor. Add the tofu, optional maple syrup, and vanilla extract and process until smooth. Pour the blended mixture into parfait glasses or any small glasses. Chill for 2 hours in the refrigerator or for 30 minutes in the freezer before serving.

TIPS

- You may find you don't need the optional sweetener or even the vanilla extract. Check by tasting the tofu mixture before adding them.
- If you like, top the mousse with sliced strawberries before serving.

COCONUT *"ice cream"*

$1.25 PER SERVING | **MAKES 4 SERVINGS**

Your taste buds won't know the difference between this and the ice-cream parlor variety, but your waistline and wallet sure will. If you have a weakness for coconut ice cream, this version will get you through the night, and with far fewer calories and less fat.

3 bananas, frozen

1 can (15 ounces) **light coconut milk**

1 cup unsweetened flaked coconut, plus ¼ cup for garnish

1 tablespoon maple syrup (optional)

1 tablespoon vanilla extract

Put the bananas, coconut milk, 1 cup of the coconut, optional maple syrup, and vanilla extract in a blender and process until thick and creamy. Spoon into parfait dishes and sprinkle the remaining ¼ coconut flakes on top, where your taste buds will be sure to catch the intense coconut flavor. Serve immediately.

TIPS

- For a more frugal version, decrease the amount of coconut to ½ cup, blending ¼ cup with the other ingredients and garnishing with the remaining ¼ cup before serving.
- To make this dessert colder and thicker, add a few ice cubes to the mixture before blending. To make it creamier, add an extra banana.

ON-THE-GO *fruit smoothie*

MAKES 1 SERVING | **$.75** PER SERVING

As a running coach and occasional medal winner in 5K races, I'm frequently asked "Where do you get your calcium if you don't drink cow's milk?" The answer is dark leafy greens, which can be cleverly camouflaged in a fruit smoothie. This one is a quick and energizing snack or breakfast that you can carry with you.

> **2 bananas, frozen**
>
> **1 cup vanilla soymilk, rice milk, or almond milk, plus more if needed**
>
> **½ cup frozen strawberries**
>
> **2 leaves kale, stemmed and torn into pieces**

Put all the ingredients in a blender. Turn the blender on low speed and gradually increase to high speed, processing until smooth. If necessary, add additional soymilk to facilitate processing and achieve a smooth consistency.

TIPS

- Inexpensive blenders that do not have powerful motors will burn out quickly if used frequently to prepare foods with thick consistencies, such as smoothies. I use a Vitamix that I've had for twenty-five years.

- If you don't have a high-powered blender, try using a food processor to make a smoothie. In the past, food processors were not as effective as blenders for creating truly smooth consistencies. These days, however, a high-quality food processor, such as a Cuisinart, can give close to the same results.

four-ingredient SMOOTHIE

$1.50 PER SERVING | **MAKES 1 SERVING**

The key to keeping the cost of smoothies low is keeping the ingredients to a minimum. This smoothie is as simple and inexpensive as you can get.

1 banana, frozen

8 frozen pitted cherries

½ cup vanilla almond milk or soymilk

2 leaves fresh spinach or other tender greens (see tips)

Put all the ingredients in a blender. Turn the blender on low speed and gradually increase to high speed, processing until smooth.

TIPS

- For an even less-expensive smoothie, substitute ice cubes or water for the almond milk.
- Bok choy, broccoli, lettuce, or kale can be used in place of or in addition to the spinach. If the smoothie turns too green, add more dark-colored fruit, like berries, or more almond milk.

heavenly mango SMOOTHIE

MAKES 4 SERVINGS　　　　**$.50** PER SERVING

I've made smoothies for many years, and this is my all-time favorite.

> **1 mango, peeled and cut into chunks, or 1 cup frozen mango chunks**
>
> **1 banana, frozen**
>
> **½ cup vanilla soymilk**

Put all the ingredients in a blender. Turn the blender on low speed and gradually increase to high speed, processing until smooth.

TIPS

- My cooking students and my kids like this smoothie to be very thick. If you prefer a thinner smoothie, add water or ice cubes to achieve the desired consistency.

- If you are lucky enough to have a mango tree in your yard, pick enough fruit to freeze and use when the season is over. Or bargain with a neighbor who has a tree. You've hit the jackpot if you have both a banana and mango tree!

berries, bananas, and more SMOOTHIE

$.75 PER SERVING   **MAKES 4 SERVINGS**

A smoothie can be breakfast, lunch, dessert, or a snack, depending on what you put in it. If you are not a salad eater, smoothies provide a nutritious way to sneak greens into your diet.

3 bananas, frozen

1 cup fresh or frozen blueberries

1 ripe pear, cored and chopped

½ head red leaf lettuce

⅓ cup cold water, plus more if needed

Put all the ingredients in a blender. Turn the blender on low speed and gradually increase to high speed, processing until smooth. Add more water, if necessary, to achieve the desired consistency.

chocolate-almond SMOOTHIE

MAKES ABOUT 3½ CUPS (2 LARGE SERVINGS) **$.75** PER SERVING

This antioxidant-rich smoothie can be stored in the refrigerator for up to three days, though it tastes best when fresh.

2 cups cold water, or 1½ cups water plus 1 cup ice

1 banana, frozen

¼ cup almonds, or 2 tablespoons raw almond butter

2 fresh or soft dried dates, pitted (see tip)

1 tablespoon unsweetened cocoa powder

1 tablespoon ground flaxseeds

1 tablespoon hempseeds (optional)

Put all the ingredients in a blender. Turn the blender on low speed and gradually increase to high speed, processing until smooth.

TIP: If the dried dates are hard, soak them in water to cover at room temperature for 2 to 3 hours, or until soft. Drain and proceed with the recipe as directed. The soaking liquid may be used to replace an equal amount of the water.

IN-THE-RED *smoothie*

$.50 PER SERVING   **MAKES 4 SERVINGS**

Red wine is only one source of health-promoting antioxidants. This smoothie gives you another way to drink your grapes, along with other nourishing fruits.

> **1 cup ice cubes**
>
> **½ cup fresh cranberries**
>
> **½ cup red grapes**
>
> **½ cup fresh pineapple chunks, or 1 can** (4-ounce) **pineapple chunks packed in juice, undrained**
>
> **½ cup fresh or frozen raspberries**
>
> **1 tablespoon agave nectar, maple syrup, or other sweetener** (optional)

Put all the ingredients in a blender. Turn the blender on low speed and gradually increase to high speed, processing until smooth.

peanut butter SMOOTHIE

MAKES 1 SERVING — **$1.00** PER SERVING

Try this smoothie when you are on the run but want to get your "apple a day" and plenty of protein.

8 ice cubes

1 apple, cored and chopped

½ cup rice milk or soymilk

1 tablespoon unsalted natural peanut butter (chunky or smooth)

½ teaspoon vanilla extract

Put all the ingredients in a blender. Turn the blender on low speed and gradually increase to high speed, processing until smooth.

TIP: If the apple flavor is too tart, add a few pitted dates, grapes, or raisins, or a frozen banana.

POPEYE'S *secret smoothie*

$1.00 PER SERVING   **MAKES 2 SERVINGS**

Popeye inspired a generation with a memorable song ("I'm strong to the finish, 'cause I eats me spinach"), and he inspired this smoothie as well.

> **1 to 2 cups fresh spinach**
>
> **2 bananas, frozen**
>
> **½ to 1 cup water**
>
> **½ cup frozen mango chunks**
>
> **1 to 2 medjool dates, pitted** (optional)

Put all the ingredients in a blender. Turn the blender on low speed and gradually increase to high speed, processing until smooth. Add more water, if necessary, to achieve a pourable consistency. Serve immediately.

TIP: Some of my students say they freeze their bananas with the skins on and peel them when they are ready to use them. I have tried this several times, and I always do battle trying to peel off the frozen skins, ending up with more banana under my fingernails than in the smoothie. I prefer to freeze a bunch of ripe, peeled bananas in a glass container and use them as I need them. Even when I need a knife to pry apart the frozen bananas, I still find it easier than peeling away the frozen skin.

chocolate–cherries jubilee SMOOTHIE

    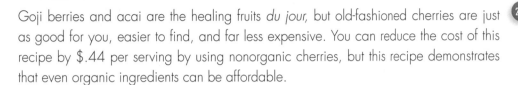

Goji berries and acai are the healing fruits *du jour,* but old-fashioned cherries are just as good for you, easier to find, and far less expensive. You can reduce the cost of this recipe by $.44 per serving by using nonorganic cherries, but this recipe demonstrates that even organic ingredients can be affordable.

> **2 bananas, frozen**
>
> **1 bag** (10 ounces) **organic frozen pitted cherries**
>
> **8 ice cubes**
>
> **1 cup vanilla soymilk**
>
> **4 teaspoons unsweetened cocoa powder**

Put the bananas, cherries, ice cubes, soymilk, and 3 teaspoons of the cocoa powder in a blender. Turn the blender on low speed and gradually increase to high speed, processing until smooth. Pour the smoothie into four glasses. Sprinkle the remaining teaspoon of the cocoa powder on the tops of the smoothies.

TIPS

- Add more ice cubes and less soymilk to reduce your cost and create a sorbet-like consistency.
- This smoothie will still be delicious if you make it without the cocoa powder.
- Add peanuts or flaxseeds for a nutty flavor and even more fiber.

PROTEIN-RICH *smoothie*

$1.50 PER SERVING — **MAKES 2 SERVINGS**

Many plant-based foods, especially seeds and nuts, are great sources of protein and calcium. In this smoothie, almonds and flaxseeds provide plenty of both.

> **2 bananas, frozen**
>
> **1 cup frozen blueberries**
>
> **½ cup raw almonds** (see tip)
>
> **¼ cup soymilk, rice milk, water, or ice cubes**
>
> **¼ cup ground flaxseeds**

Put all the ingredients in a blender. Turn the blender on low speed and gradually increase to high speed, processing until smooth.

TIP: For a creamier smoothie, if time permits, soak the almonds in water to cover at room temperature for 1 to 2 hours, then drain. Proceed with the recipe as directed.

resources

When you can't buy locally, try searching online for suppliers. A search for "grocery stores," "vegan groceries," or "vegan stores" will bring up thousands of websites. Look through the search results for stores that are close to you that offer online shopping and home delivery. These lists are always changing, so narrow your results by searching for "beans online," "grains online," or "rice online." Even Amazon carries vegan groceries. Search on their site by typing in "vegan groceries" or the specific product you want. Here are some online retailers you might find useful.

ONLINE RETAILERS

AUL Superstore • *www.aulsuperstore.com*

AUL Superstore sells standard grocery items along with a good selection of brown rice and canned beans.

Bob's Red Mill • *www.bobsredmill.com*

Order directly from Bob's Red Mill or locate a store near you that carries this line of beans, cereals, flours, and grains.

Dr. McDougall's Health and Medical Center • *www.drmcdougall.com*

Dr. McDougall's website is not only a wonderful resource for health and nutrition information, but it is also a great place to order Dr. McDougall's books and line of packaged foods.

eFood Depot • *www.efooddepot.com*

eFood Depot offers ethnic foods from all over the world, with very reasonable shipping rates.

Food Fight • *www.foodfightgrocery.com*

Food Fight is an online vegan grocery store that offers a variety of plant-based foods, including chocolate treats, pantry staples, and vegan meat alternatives.

Homeland Delivery • *www.homelanddelivery.com*

The Homeland Delivery website lists, by region, grocery stores that offer online shopping and delivery.

Jaffe Brothers • *www.organicfruitsandnuts.com*

Jaffe Brothers, in business since 1948, offers raw, untreated, and organically grown foods.

The Kushi Store • *www.kushistore.com*

The Kushi Store is affiliated with the Kushi Institute, founded by macrobiotic leader Michio Kushi. It sells a wide variety of organic beans, miso, rice, and sea vegetables.

The Mail Order Catalog • *www.healthy-eating.com*

The Mail Order Catalog carries hundreds of items, including baking supplies, dairy and meat alternatives, nut butters, soy foods, sprouting seeds, and more.

Martin Rice Online • *www.martinrice.com*

Martin Rice produces long- and medium-grain brown rice on a Missouri farm and sells at wholesale prices.

Net Grocer • *www.netgrocer.com*

Net Grocer charges a flat delivery fee (depending on where you live) of just $10. Their natural and organic section includes specialties like basmati rice, couscous, and quinoa.

Organic Kingdom • *www.organickingdom.com*

A worldwide distributor of quality organic foods and other health-related items, Organic Kingdom offers nearly four thousand organic food items and related products.

Purcell Mountain Farms • *www.purcellmountainfarms.com*

Purcell Mountain Farms sells all things beans, organic and not. The website lists 150 dried bean varieties on the home page alone. Another page has thirteen varieties of lentils, and yet another has thirteen varieties of rice.

Rancho Gordo Beans • *www.ranchogordo.com*

Reviewers consistently say that the beans sold by Rancho Gordo are so fresh, they taste better than those sold at grocery stores. Rancho Gordo also carries amaranth, quinoa, rice, and spices.

Seeds of Change • *www.seedsofchange.com*

Seeds of Change sells organic and heirloom seeds online. They also make grain mixes, pasta sauce, salad dressing, and other foods that are available only in grocery stores. However, the company offers online coupons for these products.

Simply Natural • *www.simply-natural.biz*

Simply Natural sells a wide variety of beans, grains, miso, and sea vegetables.

Sun Organic Farm • *www.sunorganic.com*

Based in California, Sun Organic Farm sells a wide range of pantry staples, including Asian foods, broth powder, nuts, and seeds.

United Buying Clubs • *www.unitedbuyingclubs.com*

United Natural Foods (UNFI) delivers food to more than three thousand buying clubs in thirty-four states that receive deliveries from UNFI's warehouses. A directory on the website helps you locate buying clubs in your area.

Vegan Essentials • *www.veganessentials.com*

Vegan Essentials is a virtual vegan department store, selling everything from clothing and shoes to food and cosmetics.

The Vegan Store • *www.veganstore.com*

The Vegan Store is a one-stop vegan shop, selling everything vegan you can eat and wear. A variety of brands are available, including Pangea, the house brand.

Additional Online Resources

To find a farmers' market in your area, visit www.ams.usda.gov/AMSv1.0/farmersmarkets.

To find a community supported agriculture (CSA) farm that offers memberships (shares) and provides locally grown produce, visit www.nal.usda.gov/afsic/pubs/csa/csa.shtml or www.localharvest.org/csa.

about the author

Ellen Jaffe Jones spent eighteen years in television news as an investigative reporter and anchor. She has won the highest awards in broadcasting, including two Emmys and first place for the National Press Club's Consumer Reporting Award. After leaving television, she earned high returns for her clients as a financial consultant at Smith Barney, where she was dedicated to socially responsible investing.

As the only healthy person in her immediate family, Ellen's passion is helping others avoid the pain and suffering she's witnessed since early childhood. Her mother, aunt, and both sisters had breast cancer. After nearly dying from a colon blockage at age twenty-eight, Ellen was told by her doctors that she needed to do things differently to avoid her family's fate.

The media have reported on the significant weight loss and improved health that Ellen's students have experienced after taking her cooking classes, which are affiliated with The Cancer Project, part of the Physicians Committee for Responsible Medicine, a national nonprofit organization. The media have also called Ellen's life "an experiment to beat the odds." She often places in 5K running races and ran her first marathon at age fifty-eight. She coaches adult running groups and is certified by the Aerobics and Fitness Association of America as a personal trainer. Ellen's weekly column, "Feasting on Fitness," appears in the *Anna Maria Island Sun*, and her monthly column, "Running Fitness," appears in the *Running Journal*. Visit Ellen's website at www.vegcoach.com.

index

Recipe titles appear in *italic* typeface.
Page references for sidebars appear in
bold typeface.

BOOK PUBLISHING COMPANY

since 1974—books that educate, inspire, and empower

To find sprouting seeds and other vegan favorites online, visit:
www.healthy-eating.com

Local Bounty

Devra Gartenstein

978-1-57067-219-4 $17.95

Becoming Vegan

*Brenda Davis, RD
Vesanto Melina, MS, RD*

978-1-57067-103-6 $19.95

Meatless Burgers

Louise Hagler

978-1-57067-087-9

Soup's On!

Barb Bloomfield

978-1-57067-047-3 $10.95

More Fabulous Beans

Barb Bloomfield

978-1-57067-146-3 $14.95

**The Simple Little Vegan
Slow Cooker**

Michelle Rivera

978-1-57067-251-4 $9.95

Purchase these health titles and cookbooks from your local bookstore or natural food store,
or you can buy them directly from:

Book Publishing Company • P.O. Box 99 • Summertown, TN 38483 • 1-800-695-2241

Please include $3.95 per book for shipping and handling.